Cycle Rides

Yorkshire Dales & the Northeast

Publisher: David Watchus
Managing Editor: Isla Love
Senior Editor: Donna Wood
Senior Designer: Kat Mead
Picture Research: Lesley Grayson
Cartographic Editor: Geoff Chapman
Cartographic Production: Anna Thompson

Produced by AA Publishing
© Automobile Association Developments Limited 2007

Published by AA Publishing (a trading name of Automobile Association Developments Limited,
whose registered office is Fanum House, Basing View, Basingstoke, Hampshire RG21 4EA;
registered number 1878835).

A03033c

ISBN-10: 0-7495-5194-1
ISBN-13: 978-0-7495-5194-0

A CIP catalogue record for this book is available from the British Library.

The contents of this book are believed correct at the time of printing. Nevertheless, the
publishers cannot be held responsible for any errors or omissions or for changes in the details
given in this book or for the consequences of any reliance on the information it provides. We
have tried to ensure accuracy in this book, but things do change and we would be grateful if
readers could advise us of any inaccuracies they may encounter. This does not affect your
statutory rights.

We have taken all reasonable steps to ensure that the cycle rides in this book are safe and
achievable by people with a reasonable level of fitness. However, all outdoor activities involve
a degree of risk and the publishers accept no responsibility for any injuries caused to readers
whilst following these cycle rides. For advice on cycling in safety, see pages 10–11.

Some of the cycle rides may appear in other AA books and publications.

Visit AA Publishing's website www.theAA.com/travel

Colour reproduction by Keene Group, Andover
Printed by in Italy by G Canale & C SPA

Cycle Rides

Contents

Locator map

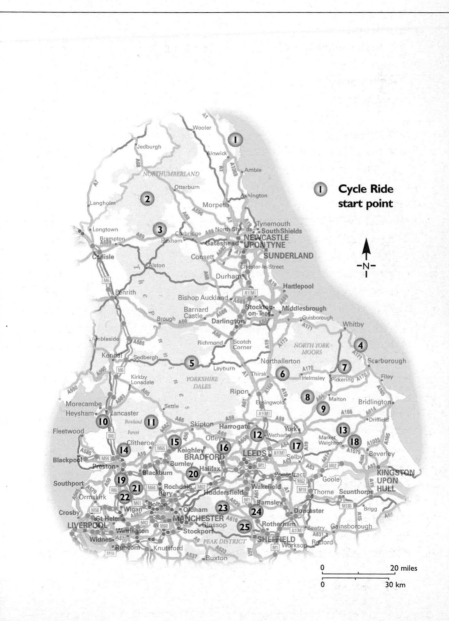

① **Cycle Ride start point**

-N-

| 0 | | 20 miles |
| 0 | | 30 km |

5

Introduction to Yorkshire Dales & the Northeast

The Yorkshire Dales receive thousands of visitors each year, most of whom are seeking peace and quiet on the moors and in the Dales. There's plenty of space for everyone, as Yorkshire and the Dales cover a large geographical area, with North Yorkshire alone claiming the title of England's largest county.

The Northeast area has plenty to offer visitors, Northumbria is a secret kingdom – a place barely discovered by tourists yet one of the most magically beautiful parts of Britain. It encompasses a vast swathe of northeast England, from the fiercely contested Scottish Border to the boundary of Yorkshire; from the High Pennines – England's last wilderness – to the golden sands along Northumberland's coast. It includes the smooth Cheviot Hills and the rugged Simonsides, deep river valleys, expansive Kielder Water and huge tracts of forest, as well as vibrant Newcastle upon Tyne, historic Durham, the long valleys of the Tees and Wear, and the fascinating

Dawn in the North York Moors National Park

country's first multi-user long-distance trail and is open to walkers and cyclists, or the lesser known Wolds Way, which has a lot of archaeological interest. At the heart of this region is the Yorkshire Dales National Park. You can cycle through countryside divided by the dry-stone walls typical of the Dales countryside, go past settlements once occupied by the Romans or cycle to York on the trackbed of the former King's Cross to Edinburgh railway line. Further north, for a spectacular route with views of the Farne Islands, head to the village of Beadnell on the Northumbrian coast. For a woodland route, try a ride through the Dalby Forest.

Many routes take in or run close to towns or villages. Hawes is known for producing crumbly Wensleydale cheese, Malham is one of the most well-visited villages in the Dales and West Burton is one of the region's prettiest villages. If you are looking to visit somewhere more out-of-the-way, Keld is one of the remoter villages. One cycle route goes to the regenerated village of Saltaire, which has stylish Salts Mill containing a gallery with works by the world-renowned Bradford-born contemporary artist David Hockney, cafés and opportunities for shopping.

There are plenty of other places to visit on route or after you've finished your ride. You can take in the impressive ruins of the priory at Bolton Abbey which are a mix of Norman and later styles, or the romantic ruins of Kirkham Priory. Castles and magnificent estates abound in Yorkshire – choose from Middleham Castle, Richmond Castle, grand Harewood House on the edge of Leeds or, the pièce de résistance, Castle Howard, which could provide an entire day's worth of entertainment including grounds, shops, a plant centre and various places to eat. Other grand buildings with beautiful gardens include Wentworth Castle and Bramham Park. Alternatively, take a trip on the North Yorkshire Moors Railway or watch extreme mountain bikers plunging down some very steep slopes in Wharncliffe Woods (joining in is optional).

industrial history of the Tyne. This region boasts many naturally occuring phenomena such as the odd geological formation near Austwick known as the erratics, and the Wensleydale waterfalls Hardraw Force (England's highest unbroken waterfall) and Aysgarth Falls.

In terms of the type of route you wish to follow, there are several 'official' trails which go through Yorkshire. Choose from the Pennine Way, the Coast-to-Coast route, the Trans-Pennine Trail, which is the

Using this book

Each cycle ride has a panel giving essential information for the cyclist, including the distance, terrain, nature of the paths, nearest public toilets and cycle hire.

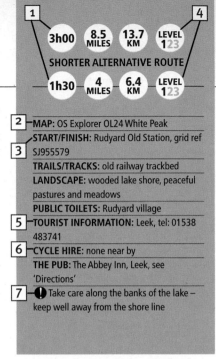

[1] **MINIMUM TIME:** The time stated for completing each ride is the estimated minimum time that a reasonably fit family group of cyclists would take to complete the circuit. This does not allow for rest or refreshment stops.

[2] **MAPS:** Each route is shown on a detailed map. However, some detail is lost because of the restrictions imposed by scale, so for this reason, we recommend that you use the maps in conjunction with a more detailed Ordnance Survey map. The relevant Ordnance Survey Explorer map appropriate for each cycle ride is listed.

[3] **START/FINISH:** Here we indicate the start location and parking area. There is a six-figure grid reference prefixed by two letters showing which 100km square of the National Grid it refers to. You'll find more information on grid references on most Ordnance Survey maps.

[4] **LEVEL OF DIFFICULTY:** The cycle rides have been graded simply (1 to 3) to give an indication of their relative difficulty. Easier routes, such as those with little total ascent, on easy footpaths or level trails, or those covering shorter distances are graded 1. The hardest routes, either because they include a lot of ascent,

greater distances, or are in hilly, more demanding terrains, are graded 3.

[5] **TOURIST INFORMATION:** The nearest tourist information office and contact number is given for further local information, in particular opening details for the attractions listed in the 'Where to go from here' section.

[6] **CYCLE HIRE:** We list, within reason, the nearest cycle hire shop/centre.

[7] ❶ Here we highlight any potential difficulties or dangers along the route. At a glance you will know if the route is steep or crosses difficult terrain, or if a cycle ride is hilly, encounters a main road, or whether a mountain bike is essential for the off-road trails. If a particular cycle route is thought suitable only for older, fitter children we say so here.

About the pubs

Generally, all the pubs featured are on the cycle route. Some are close to the start/finish point, others are at the midway point, and occasionally, the recommended pub is a short drive from the start/finish point. We have included a cross-section of pubs, from homely village locals and isolated rural gems to traditional inns and upmarket country pubs which specialise in food. What they all have in common is that they serve food and welcome children.

The description of the pub is intended to convey its history and character and in the 'food' section we list a selection of dishes, which indicate the style of food available. Under 'family facilities', we say if the pub offers a children's menu or smaller portions of adult dishes, and whether the pub has a family room, high chairs, baby-changing facilities, or toys. There Is detail on the garden, terrace, and any play area.

DIRECTIONS: If the pub is very close to the start point we say see Getting to the Start. If the pub is on the route the relevant direction/map location number is given, in addition to general directions. In some cases the pub is a short drive away from the finish point, so we give detailed directions to the pub from the end of the route.

PARKING: The number of parking spaces is given. All but a few of the cycle rides start away from the pub. If the pub car park is the parking/start point, then we have been given permission by the landlord to print the fact. You should always let the landlord or a member of staff know that you are using the car park before setting off.

OPEN: If the pub is open all week we state 'daily' and if it's open throughout the day we say 'all day', otherwise we just give the days/sessions the pub is closed.

FOOD: If the pub serves food all week we state 'daily' and if food is served throughout the day we say 'all day', otherwise we just give the days/sessions when food is not served.

BREWERY/COMPANY: This is the name of the brewery to which the pub is tied or the pub company that owns it. 'Free house' means that the pub is independently owned and run.

REAL ALE: We list the regular real ales available on handpump. 'Guest beers' indicates that the pub rotates beers from a number of microbreweries.

ROOMS: We list the number of bedrooms and how many are en suite. For prices please call the pub.

Please note that pubs change hands frequently and new chefs are employed, so menu details and facilities may change at short notice. Not all the pubs featured in this guide are listed in the *AA Pub Guide*. For information on those that are, including AA-rated accommodation, and for a comprehensive selection of pubs across Britain, please refer to the *AA Pub Guide* or see the AA's website www.theAA.com

Alternative refreshment stops

At a glance you will see if there are other pubs or cafés along the route. If there are no other places on the route, we list the nearest village or town where you can find somewhere else to eat and drink.

☛ Where to go from here

Many of the routes are short and may only take a few hours. You may wish to explore the surrounding area after lunch or before tackling the route, so we have selected a few attractions with children in mind.

Cycling in safety

CYCLING

Cycling is a fun activity which children love, and teaching your child to ride a bike and going on family cycling trips are rewarding experiences. Not only is cycling a great way to travel, but as a regular form of exercise it can make an invaluable contribution to a child's health and fitness, and increase their confidence and sense of independence.

However, the growth of motor traffic has made Britain's roads increasingly dangerous and unattractive to cyclists. Cycling with children is an added responsibility and, as with everything, there is a risk when taking them out for a day's cycling. In recent years many measures have been taken to address this, including the on-going development of the National Cycle Network (8,000 miles utilising quiet lanes and traffic-free paths) and local designated off-road routes for families, such as converted railway lines, canal towpaths and forest tracks.

In devising the cycle rides in this guide, every effort has been made to use these designated cycle paths, or to link them with quiet country lanes and waymarked byways and bridleways. Unavoidably, in a few cases, some relatively busy B-roads have been used to link the quieter, more attractive routes.

Rules of the road
- Ride in single file on narrow and busy roads.
- Be alert, look and listen for traffic, especially on narrow lanes and blind bends and be extra careful when descending steep hills, as loose gravel can lead to an accident.
- In wet weather make sure you keep a good distance between you and other riders.
- Make sure you indicate your intentions clearly.
- Brush up on *The Highway Code* before venturing out on to the road.

Off-road safety code of conduct
- Only ride where you know it is legal to do so. It is forbidden to cycle on public footpaths, marked in yellow. The only 'rights of way' open to cyclists are bridleways (blue markers) and unsurfaced tracks, known as byways, which are open to all traffic and waymarked in red.
- Canal towpaths: you need a permit to cycle on some stretches of towpath (www.waterscape.com). Remember that access paths can be steep and slippery and always get off and push your bike under low bridges and by locks.
- Always yield to walkers and horses, giving adequate warning of your approach.
- Don't expect to cycle at high speeds.
- Keep to the main trail to avoid any unnecessary erosion to the area beside the trail and to prevent skidding, especially if it is wet.
- Remember the Country Code.

Cycling with children
Children can use a child seat from the age of eight months, or from the time they can hold themselves upright. There are a number of child seats available which fit on the front or rear of a bike and towable two-seat trailers are worth investigating. 'Trailer bicycles', suitable for five- to ten-

year-olds, can be attached to the rear of an adult's bike, so that the adult has control, allowing the child to pedal if he/she wishes. Family cycling can be made easier by using a tandem, as it can carry a child seat and tow trailers. 'Kiddy-cranks' for shorter legs can be fitted to the rear seat tube, enabling either parent to take their child out cycling. With older children it is better to purchase the right size bike rather than one that is too big, as an oversized bike will be difficult to control, and potentially dangerous.

Preparing your bicycle

A basic routine includes checking the wheels for broken spokes or excess play in the bearings, and checking the tyres for punctures, undue wear and the correct tyre pressures. Ensure that the brake blocks are firmly in place and not worn, and that cables are not frayed or too slack. Lubricate hubs, pedals, gear mechanisms and cables. Make sure you have a pump, a bell, a rear rack to carry panniers and, if cycling at night, a set of working lights.

Preparing yourself

Equipping the family with cycling clothing need not be an expensive exercise. Comfort is the key when considering what to wear. Essential items for well-being on a bike are padded cycling shorts, warm stretch leggings (avoid tight-fitting and seamed trousers like jeans or baggy tracksuit trousers that may become caught in the chain), stiff-soled training shoes, and a wind and waterproof jacket. Fingerless gloves will add to your comfort.

A cycling helmet provides essential protection if you fall off your bike, so they are particularly recommended for young children learning to cycle.

Wrap your child up with several layers in colder weather. Make sure you and those with you are easily visible by car drivers and other road users, by wearing light-coloured or luminous clothing in daylight and reflective strips or sashes in failing light and when it is dark.

What to take with you

Invest in a pair of medium-sized panniers (rucksacks are unwieldy and can affect balance) to carry the necessary gear for you and your family for the day. Take extra clothes with you, the amount depending on the season, and always pack a light wind/waterproof jacket. Carry a basic tool kit (tyre levers, adjustable spanner, a small screwdriver, puncture repair kit, a set of Allen keys) and practical spares, such as an inner tube, a universal brake/gear cable, and a selection of nuts and bolts. Also, always take a pump and a strong lock.

Cycling, especially in hilly terrain and off-road, saps energy, so take enough food and drink for your outing. Always carry plenty of water, especially in hot and humid weather conditions. Consume high-energy snacks like cereal bars, cake or fruits, eating little and often to combat feeling weak and tired. Remember that children get thirsty (and hungry) much more quickly than adults so always have food and diluted juices available for them.

And finally, the most important advice of all—enjoy yourselves!

Northumberland Coast and the Farne Islands

This is a very pleasant ride with few hills and spectacular scenery. A little offshore from this stretch of the Northumbrian coast are the Farne Islands, with thousands of grey seals. Some of the islands are bird sanctuaries and can be visited by boat. Inner Farne, the largest of these small islands, is home to hordes of birds with one thing in mind.

Nesting seabirds

At the right time of year, the sky over the nearby Farne Islands is likely to be full of nesting seabirds such as guillemots, puffins, cormorants, shags, ducks and all manner of terns. Egg collectors caused great damage on these islands in the 19th century and the Farne Islands Association, set up in 1880, employed watchers to protect the breeding birds. The National Trust has owned the islands since 1925, and boat trips from Seahouses normally pass near enough to see the nesting sites.

the ride

1 From the church in the middle of Beadnell village, pass the Village Pantry and the Craster Arms and then follow the road round to the right to reach a T-junction. Turn left on to the B1340, which is signposted to Embleton.

2 At a crossroads, just before Swinhoe, turn right on to a minor road heading towards North Sunderland. This is a pretty country lane, almost level, with hedges on each side and meadows beyond. At a junction turn right on to 'Cycle Route 1' to Seahouses and Bamburgh.

A puffin, a common inhabitant of the Farne Islands, with a mouth full of fish

2h30 · **13 MILES** · **21 KM** · **LEVEL 123**

MAP: OS Explorer 340 Holy Island and Bamburgh

START/FINISH: Beadnell, on-street parking; grid ref: NU230292

TRAILS/TRACKS: roads and country lanes

LANDSCAPE: roads and country lanes with spectacular coastal views

PUBLIC TOILETS: Bamburgh, Church Street

TOURIST INFORMATION: Alnwick, tel: 01665 510665

CYCLE HIRE: Alnwick Cycles, 24 Narrowgate, Alnwick, tel: 01665 606738; www.alnwickcycles.co.uk

THE PUB: Beadnell Towers Hotel (Lobster Pot bar), The Wynding, Beadnell

Getting to the start

Beadnell village lies on the coast on the B1340, easily reached from the A1 between Alnwick and Berwick-upon-Tweed.

Why do this cycle ride?

A superb introduction to the Northumbrian coast. The fairly flat coastal roads and country lanes make for easy riding, and the views over the sea towards the Farne islands, as well as sudden glimpses of beautiful Bamburgh Castle, make this ride a truly memorable one.

Researched and written by: Hugh Taylor

The large square Norman keep of Bamburgh Castle with corner clock and to the right the 19th-century 'Captain's Lodgings'

3 At the point where the road to Bamburgh turns right at a junction beside some Nissan huts, keep on cycling straight ahead along an unsigned lane. At the next T-junction turn left and pass through the little hamlet of Elford. Opposite Elford Farm Touring Caravans, turn right and head towards Bamburgh.

4 Head up a hill and at the top you will get your first brief glimpse of stunning Bamburgh Castle ahead of you on the right. At the next junction, near Burton, keep to the left and follow this lane until you reach a crossroads at Glororum.

5 Turn right back on to 'Cycle Route 1', the B1341, and keep straight ahead for Bamburgh. The castle, perched on its basalt outcrop, dominates the skyline. Cycle on through Bamburgh to a T-junction. Turn right into Church Street, go downhill past the castle entrance and continue along the coast road to Seahouses.

6 Keep left and follow the signs for Beadnell. Keep right at a roundabout then go left at the next roundabout. Continue cycling along the coastal road and then take the first turning left into Beadnell. Cross the main road at the Post Office and continue past a bus shelter to return to the church in the village centre.

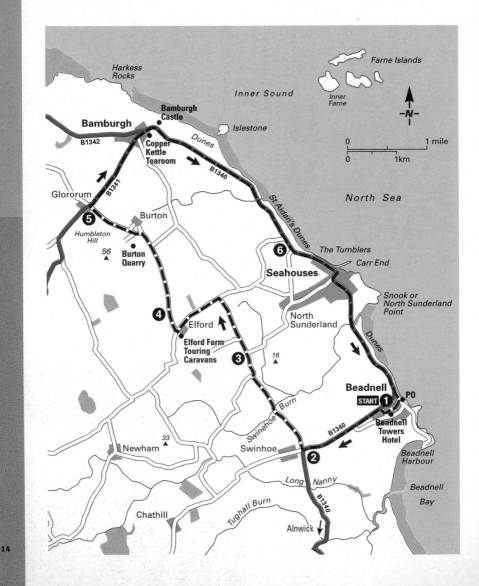

Beadnell Towers Hotel

about the pub

Beadnell Towers Hotel
Lobster Pot Bar
The Wynding, Beadnell,
Northumberland NE67 5AU
Tel: 01665 721211
www.beadnelltowers.com

DIRECTIONS: Next to Beadnell Church
PARKING: 15
OPEN: daily
FOOD: daily
BREWERY/COMPANY: free house
REAL ALE: Black Sheep, Farne Island,
Marston's Pedigree, guest beers
ROOMS: 10 en suite

Step inside the Lobster Pot bar of this hotel and you have an instant reminder that Beadnell was once an important fishing port. Memorabilia from its seafaring past festoons the walls: anchors, a ship's wheel, glass floats and scores of photographs of long dead mariners going about their daily chores. Photographs from the early 1950s show it covered in ivy, a touring car parked out front and a horse and cart ambling by. Not much has changed since. The ivy and the horse have gone but tourists' cars fill the car park and the village still exudes the atmosphere of a bygone age. The lounge running off the bar has a cosy feel with wood panelled walls, a tartan carpet and a roaring log fire.

Food
This establishment is famous for its food and can be busy. Freshly caught local seafood is a speciality with the dishes varying depending on the day's catch. The grilled sea bass and seafood Thermidor are both mouthwateringly good.

Family facilities
Families are well catered for here. There are several family rooms and a separate children's menu is available.

Alternative refreshment stops
The Copper Kettle Tearoom and the Lord Crew Hotel, Bamburgh.

☛ Where to go from here
Nearby Alnwick is a splendid market town with cosy tearooms, narrow lanes and alleys that are a delight to explore. Barter Books in the Victorian Railway Station is described as the 'British Library of secondhand books' and it has an extensive children's section. But above all, kids love visiting the castle made famous as a location in the Harry Potter films.

Both sides of the Tyne

This cycle ride takes you along both banks of the River North Tyne which has its source on Deadwater Fell in the nearby Cheviot Hills.

Where the river flows

The river flows through Europe's largest artificial lake, Kielder Water, before emerging at Falstone then flowing south to join the River South Tyne at the 'meeting of the waters' near Hexham. From here it continues as the River Tyne into the city of Newcastle. This is a very peaceful route through some splendid scenery. At Kielder Water there is a range of family-friendly activities to try, including watersports and walking trails, and at this point there is the opportunity to extend the ride on some of the many cycle trails through Kielder Forest. It is also worth spending some time exploring Falstone village. The Victorian schoolroom is part of the Tynedale Renewable Energy Trail and has been converted into an excellent tearoom, while the churchyard has several interesting gravestones from the 18th century. Look out for one depicting a girl holding hands with a skeleton. Part of the run out from Falstone takes you along the disused line of the old Borders County Railway that once ran from Riccarton Junction to Hexham.

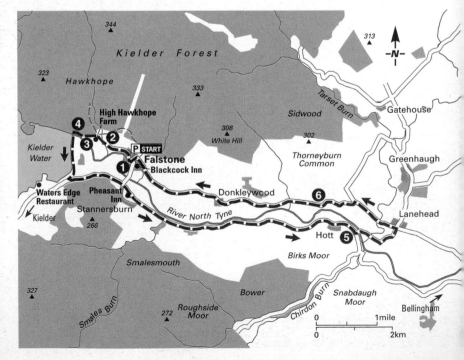

2h30 · 13 MILES · 21 KM · LEVEL 123

the ride

1 Exit the car park at the start and turn right on to a lane. Continue along it to cross a bridge by a church. The lane turns right and away from the river then forks at Mouseyhaugh. Keep left here, crossing a cattle grid, then go through a gate.

2 Cross another bridge and go through another gate then continue along the track to High Hawkhope Farm. Go through a gate and circle the right of the farmstead to reach a crossroads. Turn left on to Regional Cycle Route 10, The Reivers Route.

Kielder Water surrounded by Kielder Forest

MAP: OS Explorer OL42 Kielder Water and Forest

START/FINISH: Falstone Car Park; grid ref: NY723874

TRAILS/TRACKS: Minor roads, lanes and tracks

LANDSCAPE: forest and lakeside views

PUBLIC TOILETS: Falstone

TOURIST INFORMATION: Hexham, tel: 01434 652220

CYCLE HIRE: Kielder Castle Visitor Centre, Kielder, tel: 01434 250392

THE PUB: The Pheasant Inn, Stannersburn, Falstone (at Stannersburn, beside the minor road from Kielder Water to Bellingham)

🛈 Moderate hills, one short off-road section. Suitable for inexperienced riders as well as children

Getting to the start
Take the B6320 towards Bellingham then turn left onto a minor road signposted for Kielder. Just before Kielder Water turn right, following the signs to Falstone.

Why do this cycle ride?
This is an undemanding and tranquil route through some of Northumberland's loveliest waterside scenery. Families have the opportunity to extend their day out by trying some of the many activities on offer in and around Kielder Water, and there are many glorious cycle trails through Kielder Forest that could be used to extend this ride.

Researched and written by: Hugh Taylor

Kielder Water at sunset

3 Head uphill on this broad track passing through a forestry plantation. Just before the top of the hill the trees stop and you can see along Kielder Water. On the left is a memorial erected to commemorate the opening of the reservoir by Her Majesty the Queen on 26 May 1982.

4 Continue cycling to the top of the hill and then turn left to head down to and along the road across the dam. At a T-junction with the road turn left and keep on this route, passing the Pheasant Inn to reach the Tyne Bridge after approximately 4.5 miles (7.2km).

5 Cross the bridge and head uphill to the hamlet of Lanehead. At a junction turn left on to a narrow lane signposted to Donkleywood. This is The Reivers Route, which meanders along the edge of the Tyne valley going through several gates.The old railway track eventually disappears under water at Kielder Dam.

6 At one point you will cross over the old railway line at what was a level crossing, still with well-preserved gates. Beyond Donkleywood, climb to the highest point of the route before descending into Falstone. Go under a railway bridge then turn right opposite the Blackcock Inn to return to the car park at Falstone.

The Pheasant Inn

Tired and hungry cyclists will enjoy the traditional warmth and friendly atmosphere of this cosy stone-walled pub, owned by the Kershaw family since 1985. It began life as a large farmstead but for over 250 years one room was always used as a bar. Around the walls old photographs record local people engaged in long-abandoned trades and professions, and the wholesome food can be eaten alfresco in the pretty grassed courtyard with a stream running through it, in either of the bars or in the restaurant, with its pine furniture.

Food

The bar menu changes daily according to the season, but traditional favourites like home-made soups, steak and kidney pie, lasagne, freshly prepared sandwiches, ploughman's lunch and salads are always available. Sample dishes from the blackboard may include farmhouse paté with toast or avocado filled with grapefruit and Stilton. Main courses, in addition to roast Northumbrian lamb with rosemary and redcurrant jus, usually include a fish dish or two, and desserts might include luscious sticky toffee pudding.

Family facilities

Families with children are made very welcome but there is no separate menu.

Alternative refreshment stops

The Blackcock Inn, Falstone; Falstone Old School Tea Room; The Water's Edge Restaurant at Tower Knowe Visitors Centre, Kielder Water.

☛ Where to go from here

Wallington Hall near Rothbury is a National Trust property from the 17th century with collections of paintings, ceramics and dolls' houses. The Central Hall, reminiscent of an Italian courtyard, houses the famous series of paintings of Border history by the Pre-Raphaelite artist William Bell Scott.

about the pub

The Pheasant Inn
Stannersburn, Falstone,
Northumberland NE48 1DD
Tel: 01434 240382
www.the pheasantinn.com

DIRECTIONS: see Getting to the start

PARKING: 30

OPEN: daily

FOOD: daily

BREWERY/COMPANY: free house

REAL ALE: Marston's Pedigree, Timothy Taylor Landlord, Greene King Old Speckled Hen, Theakston's Best

ROOMS: 10 en suite

Around Hadrian's Wall and the Stanegate

This cycle route takes you along the finest section of Hadrian's Wall, past two Roman forts and along an ancient Roman road. The Wall became a World Heritage Site in 1987 and in 2005 the name was changed to the Frontiers of the Roman Empire WHS.

Roman remains

The Roman Empire had conquered as far as Mons Graupius in Northern Scotland by AD 83 but, unable to hold their gains, the Roman army gradually withdrew to a line stretching from the Solway Firth to the Tyne. There they built a line of forts along the road known since medieval times as the Stanegate. When the Roman emperor Hadrian came to power he decided to consolidate his empire and had a wall built close to the line of the Stanegate to 'separate the Romans from the Barbarians', that is, the Scots who would not accept Roman dominion.

the ride

1 Exit the car park and turn left. At a T-junction turn right on to the B6318. (A turn almost immediately to the left heads uphill to reach a car park at Steel Rigg, where a footpath leads walkers along one of the finest sections of Hadrian's Wall.)

Bottom: Hadrian's Wall

2h00 · **12 MILES** · **19 KM** · **LEVEL 1 2 3**

2 Continue along the B6318. This is a straight, undulating road with a superb view of the Wall on your left. After cycling approximately 2 miles (3.2km) pass a turn-off signed for Bardon Mill on your right and in another 0.5 mile (800m) pass the car park for Housesteads fort.

3 Housesteads is the most complete Roman fort in Britain and you may want to spend some time exploring here. Afterwards continue along the road for another 1.7 miles (2.7km) then turn right at a sign for Haydon Bridge. The building on the corner here has a tea room and is built on the site of a Roman signal station.

4 Head along this narrow lane, cycling downhill at first, followed by a short,

MAP: OS Explorer OL43 Hadrian's Wall

START/FINISH: National Park Visitor Centre car park (fee payable) at Once Brewed; grid ref: NY752668

TRAILS/TRACKS: roads and country lanes

LANDSCAPE: open and hilly, magnificent views

PUBLIC TOILETS: at the start

TOURIST INFORMATION: Hexham, tel: 01434 652220

CYCLE HIRE: Eden's Lawn Cycle Hire, Haltwhistle, tel: 01434 320443

THE PUB: Twice Brewed Inn, Once Brewed, Bardon Mill (on the B6318 just along from the Visitor Centre).

❶ Moderate incline, no off-road sections. Suitable for children and riders of all abilities. This route is very busy with walkers and other cyclists in summer

Getting to the start

The National Park Visitor Centre car park is just off the B6318 at Once Brewed (off the A69 east of Haltwhistle).

Why do this cycle ride?

A superb introduction to the awesome Roman fortifications of Northumbria. This ride takes in Housesteads Fort, one of the most visited on the Wall. Along the route the views of the Wall and the surrounding countryside are truly spectacular. The temptation to dismount and explore sections of the Wall will be very strong.

Researched and written by: Hugh Taylor

Hadrian's Wall NORTHUMBRIA

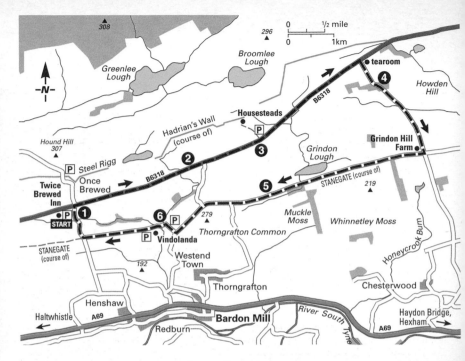

energetic pull up to the top of the next hill. Just past Grindon Hill Farm take a right turn at the crossroads on to 'Cycle Route 72', towards Bardon Mill. This is the Stanegate, an important Roman road that ran from Corbridge to Carlisle.

5 Keep ahead on 'Cycle Route 72' with a grand view of the Wall on your right and over Thorngrafton Common on your left. There is a great view of Housesteads and, further on, Vindolanda. After a downhill section turn right, still continuing on 'Cycle Route 72', following signs for Vindolanda.

6 Head downhill to reach the museum entrance. Pass by the entrance then continue uphill, passing the top car park and a thatched cottage before reaching a T-junction. Turn right on to the 'Pennine Cycle Route 68' and keep on it to reach the start of the ride once more.

Housesteads Fort, Hadrian's Wall

Twice Brewed Inn

This 17th-century coaching inn stands beside the old military road that once ran from Carlisle to Newcastle upon Tyne. It may not be one of England's most picturesque buildings but it is set amidst some of the country's finest scenery. Inside there's a warm, open-plan lounge which, like the rest of the building, is totally smoke free. There's a separate restaurant and a beer garden and although it can get busy in the summer there is usually plenty of room for everyone. It's even got its own internet café in a room just off the lounge.

Food

Most of the food is freshly prepared on the premises using fresh, local ingredients. The regional dishes like black pudding and Northumbrian sauce are particularly good. There's also a strong international theme, including dishes like nachos with salsa and guacamole. Vegetarians will enjoy the Twicey vegetable curry or the pan-fried Mediterranean veg and Halloumi cheese.

Family facilities

A separate menu ensures that children are well catered for and will find something that they like. Veggie Teddies, Turkey Dinosaurs and Snowy Owl ice cream seem to be the favourites.

Alternative refreshment stops

Cafés at Housesteads and at Vindolanda.

☛ Where to go from here

In the nearby market town of Hexham you can wander the narrow cobbled streets, visit the 7th-century abbey and its Saxon crypt, then take in the Borders History Museum, in England's oldest purpose-built jail.

about the pub

Twice Brewed Inn
Once Brewed, Bardon Mill, Hexham,
Northumberland NE47 7AN
Tel: 01434 344534
www.twicebrewedinn.co.uk

DIRECTIONS: Beside the B6318 at Once Brewed, near the National Park Visitor Centre
PARKING: 35
OPEN: daily; all day
FOOD: daily
BREWERY/COMPANY: free house
REAL ALE: Twice Brewed Bitter

Hadrian's Wall NORTHUMBRIA

23

From Ravenscar to Robin Hood's Bay

Fabulous views and a unique industrial heritage.

Alum quarries

Just after the start of the railway track proper, you pass through an area of partly overgrown spoil heaps with quarried faces above. For around two centuries, up to the Victorian era, this was an internationally important source of alum (potassium aluminium sulphate). This chemical, known since at least Roman times, had many uses, notably in the fixing of dyes. The shale rock in the cliffs was rich in aluminium sulphate and it is reckoned that over a million tons of rock were removed. The manufacturing process was centred on the alum works. The best source of potassium was seaweed; however, to complete the reaction, ammonia was required, and the

best source of this was human urine! Much of this was shipped all the way from London and off-loaded on the rocky shores directly below – a trade with some unique hazards. It's said that the proud sea-captains were reluctant to admit that they carried this undignified cargo, but if they were found out the cry would go up, 'You're taking the p**s!' It's as good an explanation as any for the origins of the phrase. You can find out more about the alum industry at the Coastal Centre in Ravenscar.

the ride

1 Descend the road until it bends sharply right. Turn left, past the **National Trust Coastal Centre**, on to an obvious descending concrete track. A rougher section needs care, but lasts less than

A collection of red-roofed stone cottages stand on the cliffs above Robin Hood's Bay

2h00	**11.25** MILES	**18.1** KM	LEVEL **1**23

MAP: OS Explorer OL27 North York Moors – Eastern

START/FINISH: roadside parking on way into Ravenscar; grid ref: NZ980015

TRAILS/TRACKS: almost entirely on well-surfaced old railway track; short street sections at Ravenscar and Robin Hood's Bay

LANDSCAPE: steep cliffs and coastal slopes, woodland and farmland, sea views

PUBLIC TOILETS: at start

TOURIST INFORMATION: Whitby, tel: 01947 602674

CYCLE HIRE: Trailways, Hawsker (about 3 miles (4.8km) from Robin Hood's Bay, on the railway route), tel: 01947 820207

THE PUB: The Laurel Inn, Robin Hood's Bay

🛈 Busy roads and car park in Robin Hood's Bay village (possible to turn round before this)

Getting to the start

Turn off the A171 about midway between Whitby and Scarborough – signed for Ravenscar. Turn left at a T-junction, then right near an old windmill. The road descends into Ravenscar and there is extensive roadside parking as the descent gets steeper.

Why do this cycle ride?

The former railway line between Whitby and Scarborough can now be followed, in its entirety, on two wheels. The full distance is 20 miles (32.2km) one way, so this ride picks out probably the finest section, looping around Robin Hood's Bay. It is a little confusing that the name of the bay and the much-photographed village are exactly the same, but the ride gives great views of the former and a chance to visit the latter.

Researched and written by: Jon Sparks

100yds (91m). Swing left through a gate on to the old **railway trackbed** and a much easier surface.

2 The track now runs below the scarred face of the **alum workings**, with some ups and downs that clearly don't match the original rail contours exactly. After this, take care crossing a **steep concrete track** that runs down to a farm.

3 Pass under an **arched bridge**. Note more quarried cliffs up on the left, while looking down to the right – if the tide is not too high – there are extensive rocky platforms in the bay, with conspicuous parallel strata. There's a short cutting and the sea views are blocked by tall gorse and broom, then it becomes more open again as the track swings gradually inland. A tall embankment

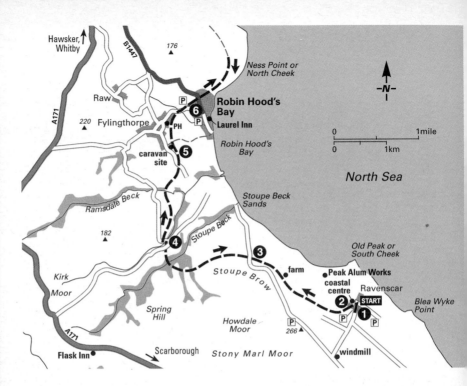

crosses a **steep wooded valley**. Carry on under a bridge and then make a sharp left turn on to a lane.

4 Go up 20yds (18m) and then sharp right to the continuation of the track. Keep right at a fork and the track resumes its steady gentle descent, then starts to turn uphill for the first time. As you come into the open after a **tunnel of trees**, the direct way ahead is again blocked (unless you're Evel Knievel!). Slant down left, cross a lane, and then climb back up on to the continuing trackbed.

5 Pass a **cricket ground**, the back of a caravan site, then a farm. Cross the rough farm track and keep straight on, through a gate where the surface changes to tarmac, on the outskirts of Robin Hood's Bay. Go through another gate and drop down to a road. Turn right down this for 100yds (91m) then left on a lane signposted to **Station**

Workshops. At the top of the rise is the old station building and just beyond it a large car park. (It is, of course, possible to descend the road all the way into the village of Robin Hood's Bay, but it's a very steep climb back. An alternative is to lock the bikes at the car park and go down on foot.)

6 Continue alongside the car park, drop down to a road, turn left and almost instantly right (very nearly straight across) on to **Mount Pleasant**. Follow this to its end then bear left up a short gravelled ride to regain the railway path. Continue for about 0.5 mile (800m). There are good views back now over Robin Hood's Bay to the cliffs near Ravenscar. Look for a National Trust sign for **Ness Bay**. There is open access on foot so you could leave the bikes and walk down to the headland, a great picnic spot. This makes as good a turn-round point as any, though the track continues into Hawsker and on to Whitby.

The Laurel Inn

The picturesque fishing village of Robin Hood's Bay is the setting for this delightful little pub. Tucked away in a row of fishermen's cottages at the bottom of the village overlooking the sea, the pub retains lots of character features, including beams and an open fire. The traditional bar is decorated with old photographs of the area, Victorian prints and brasses and an international collection of lager bottles. This coastal village was once the haunt of smugglers who used a network of underground tunnels and secret passages to bring the booty ashore.

about the pub

The Laurel Inn
New Road, Robin Hood's Bay
North Yorkshire YO22 4SE
Tel: 01947 880400

DIRECTIONS: bottom of the village
PARKING: use village car park
OPEN: daily; all day (2pm–11pm Monday to Friday November to February)
FOOD: daily; all day
BREWERY/COMPANY: free house
REAL ALE: Theakston's, John Smith's, Jennings Cumberland

Food

Bar food is limited to a simple and straightforward menu offering wholesome sandwiches and soups.

Family facilities

Due to its size there are few facilities for family groups although children are very welcome in the snug bar until 9pm.

Alternative refreshment stops

Various pubs and cafés in Robin Hood's Bay including The Victoria Hotel at the top of the village.

☛ Where to go from here

Locally, learn more about alum mining at the Peak Alum Works in Ravenscar and this fascinating coastline at the Ravenscar Coastal Centre. Children will enjoy visiting the Old Coastguard Station in Robin Hood's Bay. Head north to Whitby to see the moody and magnificent ruins of Whitby Abbey (www.english-heritage.org.uk) and visit the Captain Cook Memorial Museum (www.cookmuseumwhitby.co.uk). High on

the list for children may be the Sea Life and Marine Sanctuary in Scarborough, home to seahorses, otters, sharks, a seal hospital and convalescing sea turtles.

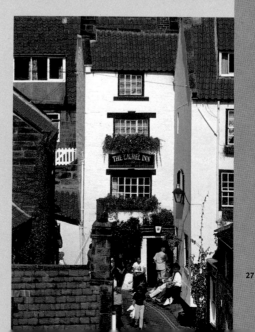

Robin Hood's Bay

NORTH YORKSHIRE

Green ways of Wensleydale

A glorious green terrace above one of the grandest of the Dales.

Bolton Castle

You hardly need to look for Bolton Castle. It dominates the landscape as you follow the road east of Carperby and towers over you as you toil up the lane of the main climb. The bulk of the castle dates back to 1399; it was established by Richard le Scrope, 1st Lord Scrope of Bolton and Lord Chancellor of England, and is still owned by his descendants. Much of the fabric is intact and there are rooms on five floors with furnishings and tableaux that give a vivid impression of what life in the castle was like. Mary Queen of Scots was imprisoned here for a time, though she was probably not too uncomfortable as she is said to have had 51 servants at her disposal! The castle grounds include a medieval garden, a herb garden and England's highest vineyard.

The old lead-mine site that is so conspicuous near the end of the off-road section is only one of many in the area, with the highest concentration being in nearby Swaledale. There is little to see in the way of buildings, shafts or levels here, just the large areas of bare spoil. The lack of vegetation colonising the ground indicates that there are probably significant residual concentrations of lead.

the ride

1 Cross the footbridge and follow a narrow tarmac path out to a wider, roughly surfaced lane. Bear right, cycle up to a road and turn right. About 2 miles (3.2km) beyond Carperby is a left turn signed for **Castle Bolton**, and the main climb of the route. Pass close under the corner of one of the **towers** and then at the top turn left, following signs for the car park and toilets.

2 Where the lane swings up into the car park, keep straight ahead through a gate and along an easy track. Follow the track through several gates and skirt to the left of some large **wooden farm sheds**; there can be muddy splashes here. After the next gate, the track becomes a little rougher, wiggling left through another gate and then right again. The track beyond is distinctly rougher, especially where it

14th-century Bolton Castle is visible on parts of the route

dips at a small **ford**; some people may prefer to walk this short section.

3 At the next gate bear left above the wall, on easygoing grass with some wheel ruts and a few avoidable rocky patches. After some perfect, almost lawn-like grass, dip to a ford, sometimes dry but still quite rough. More good grassy going follows. At the next gate bear half left on a smooth green track, following signs to Askrigg and Carperby, which gives delightful easy riding for the next 0.5 mile (800m) to **Low Gate**.

4 At Low Gate go straight ahead up the hill on more smooth green track, signed for Askrigg. Level out and descend to a gate where a rougher track (**Peatmoor Lane**) crosses. Follow the green track ahead, across a level grassy plateau, until it descends to **Oxclose Gate**. From here the track skirts to the left of the conspicuous bare ground and spoil heaps on the site of the **old lead mine**.

5 Opposite this the track acquires a good gritty surface, and soon swings down to a gate, with a **ford** just beyond. Wheel the bikes across this and beware the drop just below. Follow the stony track through another gate. Beyond this a short section is sometimes wet but can be avoided by skirting to the right, crossing ruined walls. Go up to another gate, swing left through it and down 50yds (45.7m) to a signpost.

6 For the shorter loop, descend the steep, twisting track to the little village of **Woodhall**. The surface is loose in places, and inexperienced riders should walk

2h00 · **12.5 MILES** · **20.1 KM** · **LEVEL 123**

SHORTER ALTERNATIVE ROUTE

1h30 · **9.75 MILES** · **15.7 KM** · **LEVEL 123**

MAP: OS Explorer OL30 Yorkshire Dales – Northern & Central

START/FINISH: small car park on A684 at Aysgarth; grid ref: SD995889

TRAILS/TRACKS: good grassy tracks; a few short rough sections to be walked; return on lanes which are muddy after rain

LANDSCAPE: high pasture and moorland with views of broad pastoral dale

PUBLIC TOILETS: at Bolton Castle car park

TOURIST INFORMATION: Aysgarth Falls National Park Centre, tel: 01969 663424

CYCLE HIRE: none locally

THE PUB: The Wheatsheaf Hotel, Carperby

❶ Basic loop: steep climb on road, short sections of rough track, steep descent – mountain bike recommended. Off-road sections on longer loop are considerably rougher and only for older, experienced children – mountain bike essential

Getting to the start

Aysgarth is on the main A684 road through Wensleydale. Parking by arched footbridge about 0.5 mile (800m) west of the village.

Why do this cycle ride?

Persevere as far as Low Gate and the real worth of this ride becomes apparent. From here on, you follow a magical green ribbon of a bridleway along a broad terrace high above the valley. Then you crest another slight rise and more smooth grassy trails unfurl ahead. When you get back to tarmac, it's downhill nearly all the way.

Researched and written by: Jon Sparks

Wensleydale NORTH YORKSHIRE

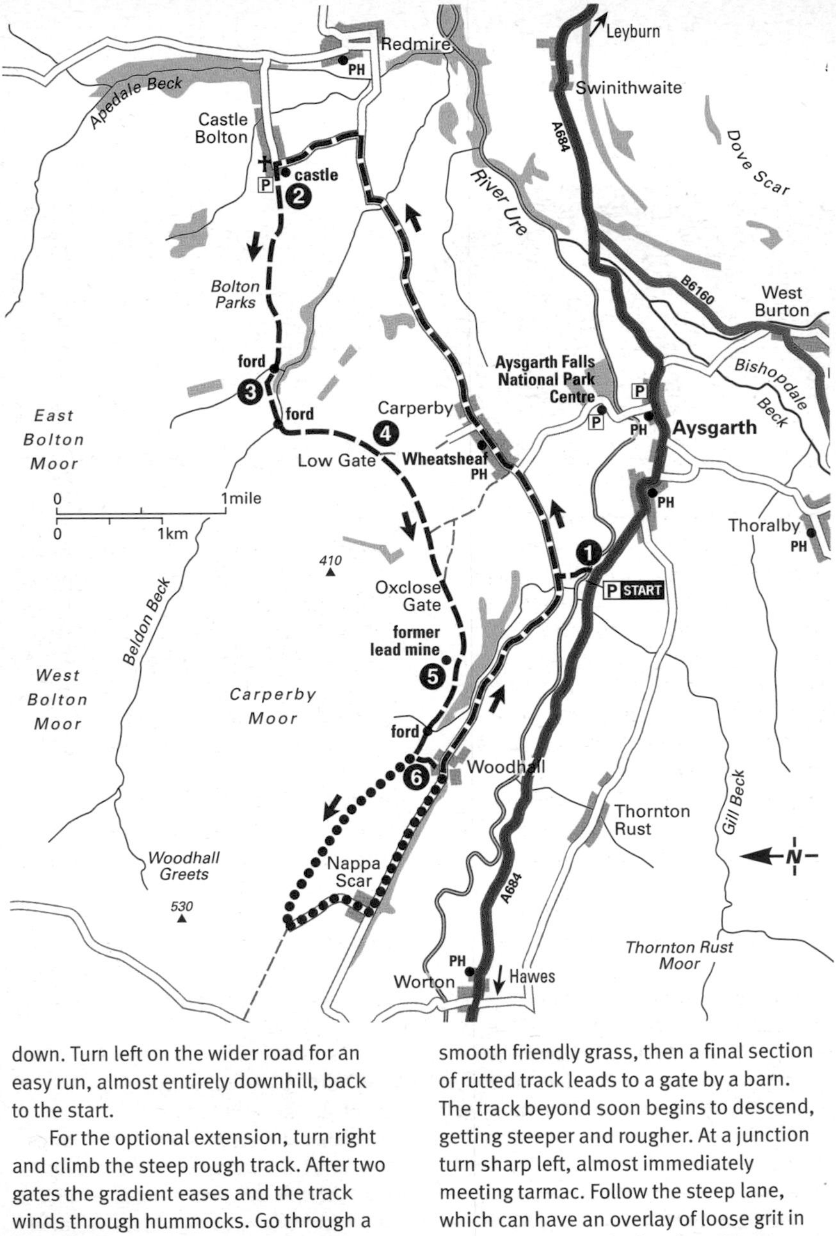

Map labels:

Leyburn

Redmire
PH
Swinithwaite

Apedale Beck

Castle
Bolton

Dove Scar

A684

† castle
P
2

River Ure

B6160

West
Burton

Bolton
Parks

Aysgarth Falls
National Park
Centre
P

Bishopdale Beck

ford
3

ford

Carperby

P
PH
Aysgarth

East
Bolton
Moor

4

Low Gate
Wheatsheaf
PH

PH

Thoralby
PH

0 ___ 1mile
0 ___ 1km

1

P START

410 ▲

Oxclose
Gate

Beldon Beck

former
lead mine
5

West
Bolton
Moor

Carperby
Moor

ford
6
Woodhall

Thornton
Rust

Gill Beck

←N→

Woodhall
Greets

530 ▲

Nappa
Scar

Thornton Rust
Moor

A684

PH
Worton

Hawes

---

down. Turn left on the wider road for an easy run, almost entirely downhill, back to the start.

For the optional extension, turn right and climb the steep rough track. After two gates the gradient eases and the track winds through hummocks. Go through a gate alongside a **small plantation**. Beyond is the final climb, very tricky in places with bare rock and large loose stones; only experts will ride it all. Over the top there's smooth friendly grass, then a final section of rutted track leads to a gate by a barn. The track beyond soon begins to descend, getting steeper and rougher. At a junction turn sharp left, almost immediately meeting tarmac. Follow the steep lane, which can have an overlay of loose grit in places, down into the hamlet of **Nappa Scar** and turn left on to the wider road.

The Wheatsheaf Hotel

about the pub

The Wheatsheaf Hotel
Carperby, Leyburn
North Yorkshire DL8 4DF
Tel: 01969 663216
www.wheatsheafinwensleydale.co.uk

DIRECTIONS: village signposted off the A684 at Aysgarth
PARKING: 20
OPEN: daily; all day Saturday and Sunday; closed Monday lunchtime in winter
FOOD: daily
BREWERY/COMPANY: Black Sheep Brewery
REAL ALE: Black Sheep Best & Special, Websters Yorkshire Bitter
ROOMS: 12 en suite

The Wheatsheaf is quietly proud of a couple of its more famous guests. In 1941 it was the honeymoon location for Alf Wight – rather better known as 'James Herriot' of All Creatures Great and Small fame. The following year it played host to an even more famous visitor in the shape of Greta Garbo, then performing a few miles away at Catterick Garrison. Garbo's legendary wish of 'I want to be alone' might be satisfied on the expansive moors above rather than in the sociable bar or the adjoining snug – which truly lives up to its name.

There is also a panelled dining room, and while you're there, do take a peek into the residents' lounge with its magnificent 17th-century fireplace. When the weather permits, there is outside seating at the front (south-facing) and there are more tables tucked in among shrubs and conifers behind the car park.

Food

Home-made dishes on the bar menu include giant Yorkshire puddings with various fillings, leek and parsnip hotpot, steak and bacon pie, Kilnsey trout with almonds, in addition to sandwiches and ploughman's lunches.

Family facilities

Children are welcome in the pub and overnight (one family room), and there's a children's menu.

Alternative refreshment stops

There's the George & Dragon in Aysgarth village and a café at Aysgarth Falls National Park Visitor Centre.

☞ Where to go from here

Stop off at nearby Bolton Castle (www.boltoncastle.co.uk); head for Hawes to visit the fascinating Dales Countryside Museum (www.destinationdales.org.uk); watch traditional ropemaking at the Hawes Ropemaker (www.ropemakers.co.uk); or learn about cheese-making at the Wensleydale Cheese Experience (www.wensleydale-creamery.co.uk).

The Hambleton Hills

An exciting ride on the top of the moors.

Hambleton Hills

The long tarmac lane that takes you north from Sutton Bank seems unremarkable in itself, but there's a history, dating back to the Iron Age tribes who settled here around 400 BC. They would have used this road long before the Romans followed in their footsteps. Evidence of the tribes' existence is all around you, from the burial tumuli near the escarpment's edge to a 60 acre (24.3ha) fort on Roulston Scar. Strangely, there are no traces of any hut circles within the fort's huge ramparts. It is possible that this was a temporary bastion in times of war, but it could also have been a huge cattle corral for neighbouring settlements.

Hambleton has many connections with beasts of burden. When the Great North Road became a turnpike the Scottish cattle drovers turned to the hills to avoid the tolls. The previously mentioned road became

known as the Hambleton Drove Road, a busy highway with several drovers' inns along the way. Hereabouts there were two – one, Dialstone House, is now a farm, but the other, the Hambleton Hotel, remains an inn.

Hambleton has long been associated with racehorses. In 1740 an Act of Parliament decreed that horse-racing could only take place at Hambleton, York and Newmarket. Fifteen years later, however, the racecourse was closed, but nearby Hambleton House remains to this day a well-known training stable for thoroughbreds.

the ride

1 Before you leave the centre, take a look at the panoramas to the south and west, for you can see for miles across the flat fields of the Vales of Mowbray and York. Alf Wight, alias the fictional vet James Herriot, believed this view to be the finest in England. Apparently, both York Minster and Lincoln Cathedral are discernible on a clear day. From the visitor centre car park, turn left up

the lane signed to Cold Kirby and Old Byland. Take the left fork past **Dialstone Farm** and its tall **communications mast**, before heading north on an ever-so-straight lane through cornfields and pastures.

2 The lane comes to a T-junction by a triangular wood, the **Snack Yate Plantation**. This is a popular starting point for serious mountain bikers who will swoop down on rough tracks through Boltby Forest. Your route turns left down the lane. It's a gentle downhill for a short distance. Just before the road dives off the edge, turn left through a gate on to a grassy bridleway along the escarpment's edge. You're riding on the Hambleton Hills. The first stretch is slightly uphill, but the track is firm and the views wide-sweeping. You'll see a small **reservoir** surrounded by forestry and the village of **Boltby** huddled under a pastured hill.

3 The bridleway climbs to the top of the hill at **High Barn**, an old stone ruin shaded by a fine stand of sycamore. The going eases and the cliffs of an **old quarry** appear ahead. Here the bridleway goes through a gate on to a walled track for a short way. Ignore the bridleway on the left, which goes back to the Hambleton Road, and stay with the edge path to the hill above the rocks of **Boltby Scar**. This is the highest point of the ride. Note the wind-warped larch trees around here – they add to the views over the edge and across the expansive Vale of Mowbray.

4 The trees of the **Boltby Forest** now cover the west slopes, almost to the summit.

The countryside near Boltby Forest

2h00 · **7.4 MILES** · **12 KM** · **LEVEL 123**

MAP: OS Explorer OL26 North York Moors – Western
START/FINISH: Sutton Bank Visitor Centre; grid ref: SE516831
TRAILS/TRACKS: good level lanes followed by undulating bridleways on the escarpment's edge
LANDSCAPE: pastoral plateau and moorland ridge
PUBLIC TOILETS: Sutton Bank Visitor Centre
TOURIST INFORMATION: Sutton Bank Visitor Centre, tel: 01845 597426 (weekends only Jan– Feb)
CYCLE HIRE: none locally
THE PUB: The Hambleton Inn, Sutton Bank
❶ A short section near Point 5 becomes narrower and with a few rocks in places. Inexperienced cyclists should dismount

Getting to the start
Sutton Bank is 6 miles (9.7km) east of Thirsk. Take the A170 Scarborough turn-off from the A19 at Thirsk. This climbs the difficult road to Sutton Bank (caravans prohibited). The centre and car park are on the left at the top.

Why do this cycle ride?
You can enjoy some of the north of England's best views and feel a sense of excitement and adventure with a ride on the 'edge'.

Researched and written by: John Gillham

Hambleton Hills NORTH YORKSHIRE

33

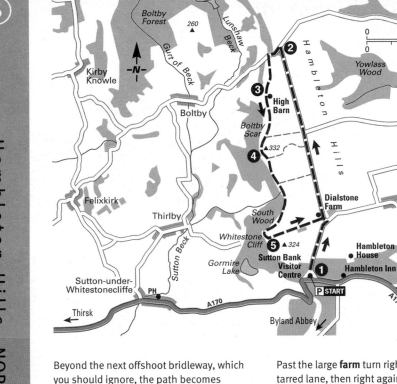

Beyond the next offshoot bridleway, which you should ignore, the path becomes narrower, with a few embedded rocks in places. The difficulties are short-lived, but the younger and less experienced riders might prefer to dismount. The riding gets easier again as the bridleway arcs right above **South Wood**. At the end of this arc you turn left to a sign that tells you that the continuing edge path is for walkers only. This is a fine spot to linger and admire the views. To the south the half-moon-shaped **Gormire Lake** lies in a nest of broad-leaved woodland and beneath the sandy-coloured **Whitestone Cliff**.

5 When you've rested, turn left on a bridleway to **Dialstone Farm**. This heads east across large prairie-like fields. Beyond a wood, the **High Quarry Plantation**, you'll see the hurdles of the **equestrian centre**.

Past the large **farm** turn right along the tarred lane, then right again, back to the visitor centre car park.

A cyclist takes a track near Boltby Forest

The Hambleton Inn

about the pub

The Hambleton Inn
Sutton Bank, Thirsk
North Yorkshire YO7 2HA
Tel: 01845 597202

DIRECTIONS: beside the A170 Thirsk to Scarborough road, at the top of Sutton Bank

PARKING: 50

OPEN: daily in season; phone ahead

FOOD: daily

BREWERY/COMPANY: free house

REAL ALE: Black Sheep, local Hambleton ales

Just a few hundred yards from the Sutton Bank edge and those famous James Herriot views, The Hambleton Inn is backed up by sprucewoods. It's an extremely popular pub with walkers and cyclists. The whitewashed Georgian building was once frequented by cattle drovers, who herded their beasts across the high Hambleton Drove Road. The inn has a large lawned garden to the rear, and flagged patios to the front and sides. Expect an enthusiastic and extremely friendly service, imaginative pub food, summer hog roasts and live entertainment.

Food
Food is freshly prepared and a cut above the pub norm. Snacks include a traditional ploughman's lunch and baked baguettes (crab and lemon mayonnaise, roast ham and pickle), while more substantial bar meals range from beefburger and chips and deep-fried Whitby haddock and chips to bangers and mash, and pasta with poached salmon and lemon and watercress sauce. There's a separate evening menu.

Family facilities
The pub is really geared up for families. Children are very welcome inside the pub where an above-average children's menu is available for younger family members, as well as smaller portions of adult dishes. When the weather's fine there's good patio seating and a large lawned area with play area to keep children amused.

Alternative refreshment stops
Café at Sutton Bank Visitor Centre.

☛ Where to go from here
Visit nearby Rievaulx Abbey (www.english-heritage.org.uk), once the most important Cistercian abbey in Britain; the soaring ruins are powerfully atmospheric in the beautiful Rye valley. Another evocative ruin to explore is Byland Abbey at the base of the Hambleton Hills, or head east to Pickering to take a steam railway journey through stunning scenery on the North Yorkshire Moors Railway (www.northyorkshiremoorsrailway.com).

Hambleton Hills NORTH YORKSHIRE

Dalby Forest

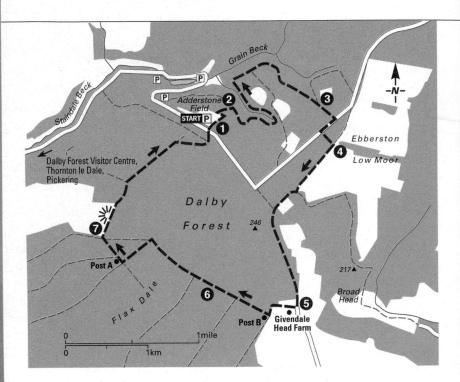

A short ride through the forest where you seek the wildlife that's watching you.

The Forest

In 1919, when the Forestry Commission was founded, Britain's woodland cover had shrunk to around 5 per cent, which meant we had to import large quantities of timber to meet the increasing needs of industry. In Yorkshire they turned to Dalby on the southeast corner of the North York Moors. The area, once part of the Royal Hunting Forest of Pickering, had degenerated into boggy heathland, poverty-stricken

upland farms and a huge rabbit warren that provided fur for a felt hat industry. Several streams drained the moorland plateau and flowed south west into Dalby Beck, forming a rigg and dale landscape. Scrub oak and birch clustered around these streams, but in general the ground was only suitable for conifers. By 1921 the planting began and within years over 8,500 acres (3,442ha) of Sitka Spruce and Scots Pine had covered the ground.

Conservationists hated these new forests, complaining that wildlife had been decimated, but today, if you stay quiet and look hard enough, you'll see that it's really quite abundant. In quieter corners you may stumble upon the Bambi-like roe deer. Many of the mammals, such as the pygmy shrew and the otter, stay clear of humans and it's bird-life you're more likely to spot. Besides the common blue tits, you're quite likely to see a wading heron, or a tiny warbler such as that summer visitor, the chiffchaf, so called because of its birdsong.

the ride

1 The **green cycle route** begins beyond the trees at the southeast end of the large **Adderstone Field** (the furthest from the visitor centre). Here you turn left along a narrow slightly downhill track. Though still easy, it's the most difficult section of the route – use gentle braking if you're a little unsure. Ignore two lesser, unsigned left fork tracks.

2 Turn right along a much wider forestry track which takes a winding course round the afforested valley of **Worry Gill**. Where the more demanding red route goes off on a rough track to the right, your green route goes straight on, still using a well-graded track.

3 Where a track doubles back, go straight on up a steady hill before meeting the **forest drive** again. Cross this with care – it can be quite busy on summer weekends – before turning right along it for 200yds (183m). Turn left along a narrow path signed with red and green waymarkers and just before a 30 mile per hour speed limit sign (hope you were not speeding!). If you're early and it's summer, you may be able to dally and eat some of the bilberries that grow beside the path.

2h00 · **6 MILES** · **9.7 KM** · **LEVEL 1 2 3**

MAP: OS Explorer OL27 North York Moors Eastern Area

START/FINISH: car park at Adderstone Field, Dalby Forest; grid ref: SE883897

TRAILS/TRACKS: forestry roads and a few narrow paths, mostly well graded

LANDSCAPE: conifer forest

PUBLIC TOILETS: Visitor Centre, Lower Dalby (not on route)

TOURIST INFORMATION: Dalby Forest Visitor Centre, tel: 01751 460295

CYCLE HIRE: Cycle Hire Kiosk next to Visitor Centre, Low Dalby, tel: 01751 460400

THE PUB: New Inn, Thornton le Dale, off the route

🅘 There's a short, rough and slightly downhill section of track at the start. The forest drive road needs to be crossed with care twice

Getting to the start
From the A170 at Thornton le Dale head north on a minor road signed the Dalby Forest, then turn off right on the Dalby Forest Drive, where you'll come to the tollbooths. Adderstone Field, the start of the ride, lies about 5 miles (8km) beyond the visitor centre.

Why do this cycle ride?
It's a good introduction to forest tracks, with just a few hilly bits to get your pulse racing, but nothing frightening to put off the inexperienced. There's lots of wildlife for the observant cyclist.

Researched and written by: John Gillham

4 The path reaches a **flinted road** at the south east edge of the forest. Turn right along this then left at the next junction. Looking left, you'll see the rougher high pastures of **Ebberston Low Moor** decline to the greener, more fertile fields of the **Vale of Pickering**.

5 Turn right just before reaching **Givendale Head Farm** along a rutted farm track with a grassy island in the middle. Turn right at the next junction (**Post B**) on a downhill section, followed by an uphill one where you're joined by a **farm track** from the left.

6 A long hill follows to a wide junction where you go straight on along a tarred lane. A sign tells you that you're now at the head of **Flaxdale**. Stay with the tarred lane at the next bend and junction. Turn right at the crossroads along a long sandy track

(**Post A**), then right again at the next junction. Note the **linear earthwork** to both left and right – nobody seems to know the exact origins of these.

7 After going straight on at the next junction past a fine stand of **Scots pines**, you get fine views over the farm pastures of High Rigg to **Levisham Moor**. There's another downhill section followed by an uphill one. Take a right fork at **Newclose Rigg**. Where the red route goes straight on, your green route veers right along the main track. There's a downhill left curve beyond which you take the **upper right fork**, which brings the route back to the forest drive opposite Adderstone Field.

Top: A track in Dalby Forest

New Inn

7

A Georgian coaching inn in the centre of a picturesque village complete with beck running beside the main street, village stocks and a market cross. The inn retains its old-world charm, with log fires, a low beamed ceiling, traditional furniture and hand-pulled ales.

Food

Freshly cooked food is one of the pub's attractions, with many tempting choices on the interesting menu and specials board: salmon and prawn filo parcels with creme fraiche, chicken in red wine sauce and beef Madras with rice and mini popadoms show the range of main courses.

Family facilities

Children are welcome in the dining area if eating. They have their own menu.

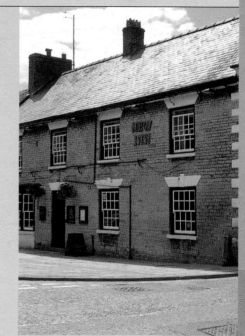

about the pub

New Inn
Maltongate, Thornton le Dale
Pickering, North Yorkshire YO18 7LF
Tel: 01751 474226

DIRECTIONS: beside the A170 in the centre of the village
PARKING: 15
OPEN: daily; all day in summer
FOOD: daily
BREWERY/COMPANY: Scottish & Newcastle
REAL ALE: Theakston's Black Bull, John Smith's, Black Sheep
ROOMS: 6 en suite

Alternative refreshment stops

There's a café and refreshment kiosk at the Dalby Forest Visitor Centre.

☞ Where to go from here

The Beck Isle Museum at Pickering houses many photos and artefacts that will show you the local customs. The museum follows the historical developments in social and domestic life of the last two centuries (www.beckislemuseum.co.uk). Re-live the golden age of steam with a ride on the North Yorkshire Moors Railway, Britain's most popular heritage railway, through 18 miles (29km) of stunning scenery (www.northyorkshiremoorsrailway.com).

Terrington and Castle Howard

A ride through Yorkshire's most magnificent estate.

Castle Howard

Six years after Henderskelfe Castle burned down in 1693, Charles Howard, the 3rd Earl of Carlisle, asked his friend, Sir John Vanbrugh, to design its replacement, Castle Howard. Vanbrugh at this time was a complete novice, though he would later design Blenheim Palace. However, he formed a successful team with Christopher Wren's clerk, Nicholas Hawksmoor. The building programme would last 100 years, the lifetime of three earls, but the legacy left Yorkshire with one of Britain's most elegant palaces, set among magnificent and colourful gardens, complete with lakes, fountains, classical statues and temples.

In the house itself, the marble entrance hall is lit subtly by a dome. Explore further and you'll see treasures built up over centuries, including antique sculptures, fine porcelain, and paintings by Rubens, Reynolds and Gainsborough. In 1940 fire came to haunt the Howards once more. A devastating blaze destroyed the dome and twenty of the rooms, leaving the palace open to the elements and in need of extremely costly renovation. That it was carried out so successfully is all down to George Howard, who inherited the estate after the death of his two brothers during World War II.

the ride

1 Terrington is a peaceful little village with fine sloping greens either side of the main street, giving the place a spacious feel. The cottages, which are largely Victorian, are built with local limestone. Above them, just off the main street, stands the church, a square-towered building that dates back to Saxon times – there's an

8

Castle Howard is set amongst 1,000 acres (405ha) of grounds and gardens

2h00 · 9.3 MILES · 15 KM · LEVEL 123

Anglo-Saxon window in the south aisle. Much of the structure is 13th-century but was modernised around 1860.

Heading east past the ivy-clad **Bay Horse Inn** towards Castle Howard is slightly downhill, a nice start – the tea rooms tempt you straight away. If it's hot, a splendid avenue of trees on the way out of the village will offer some welcome shade.

2 Take the right fork, signed 'to Ganthorpe, York', 0.5 mile (800m) out of the village. Now you pay for your downhill as the road climbs to the top of **Cross Hill**, where there's a good view back to Terrington. The lane levels out as it passes through the stone cottages and farms of **Ganthorpe**. This hamlet was the birthplace of the historian, Arthur Toynbee (1886–1975) and the botanist, Richard Spruce (1817–93), who travelled to places like the Andes and the Amazon in search of specimens for scientific research. There's another short downhill section as the lane bends right by **Sata Wood**, then it's uphill again.

3 Turn left at the T-junction, where you get glimpses of a couple of the **Castle Howard domes**, then left at the crossroads following the directions to Slingsby and Castle Howard. The road, known as the **Stray**, is straight and madly undulating like a Roman road, with wide verges and avenues of trees lining the way. Some of the traffic is speedy so take care! Soon you pass beneath the extremely narrow stone arch of the Castle Howard estate's **Carrmire Gate**, which is flanked by castellated walls, then you come upon the gate house with its pyramidal roof. There's a roundabout next to a 100ft (91m) **obelisk** of 1714 dedicated

MAP: OS Explorer 300 Howardian Hills and Malton

START/FINISH: roadside parking in the main street, Terrington; grid ref: SE670706

TRAILS/TRACKS: country lanes with some hills

LANDSCAPE: rolling pastoral hills and parkland

PUBLIC TOILETS: at Castle Howard

TOURIST INFORMATION: Malton, tel: 01653 600048

CYCLE HIRE: none locally

THE PUB: Bay Horse Inn, Terrington

❶ The hilly terrain might be a little tiring for younger children. Take care on the Stray (Point 3) – some of the traffic here is faster than it should be

Getting to the start
From the A64 north east of York, follow the signs for Castle Howard and take the first left after the castle entrance. Alternatively, from Helmsley follow the B1257 signed 'Malton' to Slingsby and turn right for Castle Howard. Turn right by the castle's Great Lake.

Why do this cycle ride?
This pleasant ride combines the sophistication of the Castle Howard Estate and the simple beauty and rural charm of the Howardian Hills.

Researched and written by: John Gillham

Terrington

NORTH YORKSHIRE

to Lady Cecilia Howard. Here you need to decide whether or not to visit the palace (highly recommended).

4 Continuing down the Stray you'll pass the **Obelisk Ponds**, which are enshrouded by woodland, then the **Great Lake**, across which you get a great view of the palace and its many domes.

5 Turn left for 'Terrington' at the crossroads just beyond the lake. The lane soon swings right and climbs through the trees of **Shaw Wood**. If you have mountain bikes and

Neatly lawned houses built from local limestone at Terrington, at the end of your ride

are experienced riders you could take the bridleway at the next bend (**South Bell Bottom**) then double back on the track over Husket and Ling Hills to meet the lane further west. If not, continue with the lane, which winds downhill across **Ganthorpe Moor** to meet the outward route by the first T-junction east of Terrington. Though you've still got the trees for shade, the downhill section is now an uphill stretch, so you'll probably deserve that refreshment stop at the **Bay Horse Inn**.

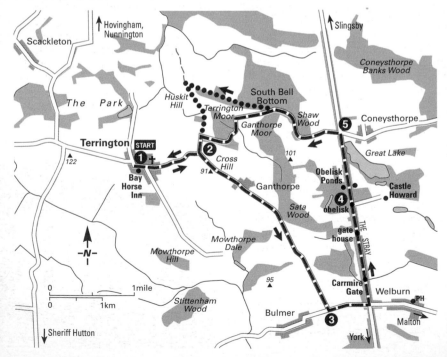

Bay Horse Inn

about the pub

Bay Horse Inn
Main Street, Terrington
Malton, North Yorkshire YO60 6PP
Tel: 01653 648416

DIRECTIONS: see Getting to the Start; pub in the village centre
PARKING: 30
OPEN: daily; all day
FOOD: daily; all day
BREWERY/COMPANY: free house
REAL ALE: Theakston's Best, John Smith's Cask, guest beers
ROOMS: none available

Terrington is an idyllic peaceful little village with stone cottages and greens, surrounded by the rolling Howardian Hills. The homely and friendly 400-year-old Bay Horse Inn, formerly a tailor's shop, reflects this rural charm from the outside to the interior. An archway of ivy surrounds the door of this whitewashed stone-built pub. Inside there's a welcoming log fire in the cosy lounge, while the public bar offers time-honoured pub games in the form of darts, dominoes, shove ha'penny and cribbage. At the back there's a conservatory adorned with old farm tools, and a small but attractively planted garden.

Food
The popular food here takes in traditional English pub bar meals with a specials board and Sunday roasts. Authentic Thai food is also available at lunch and dinner time, but booking is advisable.

Family facilities
Families are very welcome inside the pub, especially in the conservatory. There's a typical children's menu and the garden is sheltered and safe for children.

Alternative refreshment stops
Tea Rooms, Terrington (by the post office); Hayloft and Lakeside Cafés at Castle Howard; The Malt Shovel, Hovingham – a fine pub just north of Terrington.

☛ Where to go from here
Don't miss out on exploring Castle Howard and its wonderful gardens and landscaped grounds (www.castlehoward.co.uk). Near Malton is the Eden Camp Modern History Theme Museum (www.edencamp.co.uk) which tells the story of civilian life in World War II. Within reach is Nunnington Hall (www.nationaltrust.org.uk), Sherriff Hutton Castle and Yorkshire Lavender in Terrington.

Kirkham Priory and the Derwent Valley

A circular ride around the peaceful Derwent Valley.

Kirkham Priory

Sometime in the early 1120s, William L'Espec was riding by the banks of the Derwent when his horse threw him. He died instantly. Grief-stricken, his father, Lord Helmsley, founded an Augustinian monastery on the site of the accident.

The priory started as a small church in 1125, but by the middle of the 13th century fine western towers had been built and the eastern end extended. Later chapels were added, one abutting the north transept, and a second by the presbytery's south wall. The money ran out and the work was halted. Unfortunately, Kirkham's lack of size didn't save it from destruction during the Dissolution of the Monasteries, when it was laid to waste.

The main tower of the priory collapsed in 1784 during high winds, and locals took much of the masonry to build their own houses. However the remains that survive do much to stir the imagination. Today, it's a rather peaceful setting with lawns sloping down to the river and sylvan hillsides beyond. The wall of the 13th-century

The remains of Kirkham Priory

gatehouse is the centrepiece, with fine sculpted figures representing, among others, Christ, St George and the Dragon, St Bartholomew and David and Goliath. Also of note are the delicate arches of the lavatorium, set in the west wall of the cloister.

the ride

1 Westow is a pleasant little hillside village lying 0.5 mile (800m) above the River Derwent. Strangely the name originates from Wifestowe, meaning a place of women. The pub, the Blacksmith's Inn, is the centrepiece of the village as the church lies in isolation a mile (1.6km) to the north. Head north from the village centre then go left at the first junction, signed Kirkham and York. Although there's a bridleway on the right, it's usually too choked with vegetation to be of any use. It would be better to stay with the lane, passing the solitary electricity-generating **windmill** to arrive at a T-junction at the northern extremities of Howsham Wood. Turn right here, tracing the brow of **Badger Bank** high above the River Derwent. After staying fairly level along the bank, the lane makes a steady descent to reach the **Stone Trough Inn** at Kirkham.

2 From the inn the road descends steadily downhill, around a left-hand bend and past a small **car park** by the entrance to the priory, which is well worth a visit before you continue the journey. The road continues over **Kirkham Bridge**, an elegant three-arched stone structure, rebuilt in the 18th century.

2h00 — **8 MILES** — **12.9 KM** — **LEVEL 123**

MAP: OS Explorer 300 Howardian Hills and Malton
START/FINISH: roadside parking in Westow; grid ref: SE753653
TRAILS/TRACKS: all quiet country lanes
LANDSCAPE: rolling pastoral hills and a wooded valley
PUBLIC TOILETS: none on route
TOURIST INFORMATION: Malton, tel: 01653 600048
CYCLE HIRE: none locally
THE PUB: The Stone Trough Inn, Kirkham Abbey
❶ Some of the hills are fairly steep and challenging and would be tiring for young children

Getting to the start

Westow lies just off the A64 York to Malton road. Leave the A64 near Whitwell-on-the-Hill, following signs for Kirkham. Descend into the Derwent Valley past the priory. Go straight on at the junction to pass The Stone Trough Inn, turn left at the next junction, then right to reach the village centre. Park at the roadside.

Why do this cycle ride?

Here you can see the Derwent Valley at its most attractive, with great loops in the lively river, wooded hillsides, great mansions and a fascinating ancient priory.

Researched and written by: John Gillham

Derwent Valley

NORTH YORKSHIRE

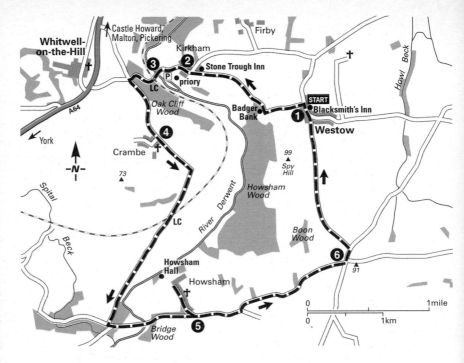

3 At the other side there's a level crossing followed by a short steep pull (you may need to dismount), as the road climbs through the dense conifers of **Oak Cliff Wood** to two closely spaced junctions. Ignore the right turns at both but instead follow signs to Crambe. The lane now follows the upper perimeter of the conifer wood before descending towards **Crambe** village.

4 This quiet backwater lies on a cul-de-sac to the right, so there's a there-and-back detour to this same spot to see the square-towered **St Michael's Church**. It's downhill from here, with a right-hand bend after 0.5 mile (800m). Beyond this you come to another **level crossing**. This one has a bell to ring to get the attention of the signalman, who will come to open it for you – it's all good 21st-century technology here in the Howardian Hills! The road descends further with the River Derwent clearly in view below left and the grand mansion of **Howsham Hall**

on the far bank. At the next T-junction turn left following the directions to 'Howsham and Leavening', but ignore the right turn shortly after. Your road crosses the Derwent at Howsham Bridge, before climbing steadily past **Bridge Wood**.

5 Howsham village lies on another cul-de-sac to the left. Its cottages have well-manicured greens; there's a small spired **church** on the right and the well-known and rather grand **Howsham Hall School** at the end of the road. Back on the main route, the lane climbs and winds over pastured knolls and after 3 miles (4.8km) comes to a high crossroads.

6 Turn left for Westow and Malton, then take the left fork for **Westow**. The road now makes a gentle ascent to a rise east of **Spy Hill**. From this elevated position all that is left of this ride is a nice and easy descent back to Westow village.

The Stone Trough Inn

about the pub

The Stone Trough Inn
Kirkham Abbey,
Whitwell-on-the-Hill,
York, North Yorkshire YO60 7JS
Tel: 01653 618713
www.stonetroughinn.co.uk

DIRECTIONS: see Getting to the start

PARKING: 100

OPEN: all day Sunday; closed Monday
except Bank Holidays

FOOD: Tuesday to Sunday

BREWERY/COMPANY: free house

REAL ALE: Tetley, Black Sheep, Timothy
Taylor Landlord, Malton Golden Chance,
Theakston's Old Peculier, guest beer

Restored in 1982 from the original Stone Trough Cottage, the Stone Trough Inn stands beside a narrow lane high above Kirkham Abbey and the River Derwent. Lots of oak beams, bare stone walls, flagged floors and cosy rooms filled with fresh flowers add colour and character, and log fires and comfortable furnishings draw a good crowd. Further attractions include the super views across the Derwent Valley and the impressive, modern pub menus that make the most of the abundant local produce available. Good global list of wines and four tip-top Yorkshire ales on tap.

Food

In the bar you'll find excellent lunchtime sandwiches (cheddar cheese and red onion), starters of warm salad of crispy chilli beef with honey and sesame seed dressing and home-made soup, and main courses such as local pork sausages on sage and onion rosti with real ale gravy, creamy fish pie, roast monkfish wrapped in Parma ham with rosemary butter sauce, and whole roast partridge with crab-apple jus. Puddings include treacle tart with vanilla ice cream. Separate restaurant menu.

Family facilities

Children of all ages are welcome. You'll find a children's menu and portions of adult dishes, high chairs, small cutlery and drawing materials to keep youngsters amused.

Alternative refreshment stops

The Blacksmith's Arms, Westow.

☛ Where to go from here

The Cistercian Rievaulx Abbey, a short way to the north, has connections with Kirkham, and is well worth seeing (www.english-heritage.org.uk). Castle Howard (www.castlehoward.co.uk) is a short drive away, as is Pickering and the North Yorkshire Moors Railway, a fascinating steam railway that travels through stunning scenery into the heart of the moor (www.northyorkshiremoorsrailway.com).

Glasson Dock to Lancaster

Follow the River Lune to explore Lancaster, and share the delights of its canal towpath on the way back.

Wildlife along the way

Aldcliffe Marsh is a Site of Special Scientific Interest because of its importance for waders such as redshank and lapwing. At one time the lapwing was a common sight on ploughed fields, but the use of insecticides and farming machinery has driven it to meadows and marshes in summer. Keep an eye open for the bright yellow ragwort, a plant that attracts the cinnabar moth, which lays its eggs on the stems and produces gaudy black-and-yellow caterpillars. In Freeman's Wood is a black poplar (*Populus nigra*), a native tree of lowland marshes and of this area, but not all that common. There are thought to be fewer than 3,000 black poplars in Britain today. The tree in Freeman's Wood is one of only two in Lancashire.

the ride

1 Begin from the large car park near the dock by crossing the road onto a cycleway along the edge of the **Lune Estuary**. A gravel track leads on to cross the River Conder before turning north through the **Conder Green car park**. (Follow the road right for The Stork pub.) Beyond the car park, ride onto a tree-lined track, and keep following this until it reaches a surfaced lane end, not far from the village of Aldcliffe.

2 Turn left into a **gravel area**, and then immediately, just before a footpath

stile, onto a broad vehicle track. At a cross-track, keep forward along a bridleway for **New Quay Road**, and going into **Freeman's Wood**. The track, now surfaced, crosses a section of **Aldcliffe Marsh**, and eventually comes out to meet a much wider road near a small light industrial complex. Keep forward until you reach an old arched bridge with the modern, **Millennium** (foot) **Bridge** near by.

3 Turn onto the footbridge, and then immediately right to leave it, without crossing the river. Go left on a surfaced **cycle lane** (signed for Halton and Caton). Follow the lane until it rises, to run briefly alongside the main road. Almost immediately turn right to perform a loop to the left into an **underpass** – you may need to dismount here. On the other side, go forward on a **signed cycle route**, which passes beneath a bridge and goes forward on a surfaced track down an avenue of trees. When it forks, keep left, and carry on to reach the stone **Lune Aqueduct**. Just before it, turn right onto a narrow path that leads to the foot of a flight of steps. Here you will need to dismount and carry your cycle up the steps to reach the towpath – a breathless few minutes, but well worth the effort.

Looking across the Lune to Lancaster

2h30 **14 MILES** **22 KM** **LEVEL 1**23

MAP: OS Explorer 296 Lancaster, Morecambe and Fleetwood

START/FINISH: Quayside, Glasson Dock; grid ref: SD446561

TRAILS/TRACKS: good route, though cyclists will need to dismount at a few points on the canal while passing waterfront pubs

LANDSCAPE: mainly old railway trackbed or canal towpaths

PUBLIC TOILETS: at the start

TOURIST INFORMATION: Lancaster, tel: 01524 32878

CYCLE HIRE: none locally

THE PUB: The Stork, Conder Green

❗ Cycles will need to be carried up and down steps to reach the canal towpath

Getting to the start

Glasson Dock is on the Lune Estuary, 4 miles (6.4km) south west of Lancaster. It is best reached from Lancaster, or Cockerham to the south, along the A588, but may also be reached from Junction 33 on the M6 via Galgate — turn left at the traffic lights in the village centre and follow signs.

Why do this cycle ride?

A superb introduction to coastal Lancashire. The old trackbed and the return along the Lancaster Canal makes for easy riding, while the traffic-free cycle route through riverside Lancaster is ingenious. You can opt out at the Millennium Bridge and explore Lancashire's ancient capital.

Researched and written by: Terry Marsh

4 Turn right along the towpath. At **Whitecross**, dismount again to change to the other side of the canal. At a couple of places now you may need to dismount again as you pass canalside pubs, but eventually a **bridge** leads back over the canal. Over the bridge, turn immediately right down steps (dismount again) to rejoin the **towpath**.

5 Continue until you pass **Bridge 95**, following which the canal has a road on the right, and bends to the left. A short way on, leave the towpath and go onto the road (near a **lodge** on the right, dated 1827). Go forward, climbing steadily into the village of **Aldcliffe**. At the top of the climb, on a bend, take care, and turn right into the first lane on the right, descending quite steeply, and continuing down past **houses**, to ride along a narrow country lane to rejoin the outward near the gravel area.

6 Turn left onto the **trackbed**, and follow this back to Conder Green, turning left into the village for **The Stork**, or continue round the coast to **Glasson Dock**.

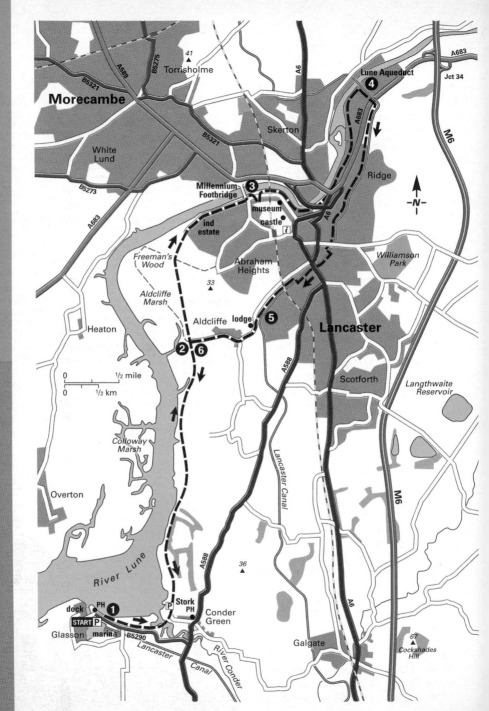

The Stork

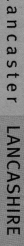

about the pub

The Stork
Conder Green, Lancaster
Lancashire LA2 0AN
Tel: 01524 751234

DIRECTIONS: just off the A558 (west), a mile (1.6km) from Glasson and the start of the ride

PARKING: 40

OPEN: daily; all day

FOOD: daily; all day Saturday & Sunday

BREWERY/COMPANY: free house

REAL ALE: Black Sheep Best, Timothy Taylor Landlord, Marston's Pedigree, guest beers

ROOMS: 10 en suite

A white-painted coaching inn spread along the banks of the estuary, where the River Conder joins the Lune estuary and just a short stroll along the Lancashire Coastal Way from the quaint seaport of Glasson Dock. The inn has a colourful 300-year history that includes several name changes. It's a friendly, bustling and ever-popular place, the draw being the location, the range of real ales, and the rambling, dark-panelled rooms, each with warming open fires. The south-facing terrace and patio look across the marshes.

Food
Seasonal specialities join home-cooked food such as steak pie, locally smoked haddock, salmon fillet with bonne femme sauce, Cumberland sausage served with onion gravy and mash.

Family facilities
Children of all ages are welcome and well catered for. There are family dining areas, family en suite accommodation, a children's menu, and a play area outside.

Alternative refreshment stops
There are plenty of cafés, restaurants and pubs in Lancaster.

☛ Where to go from here
A trip to Lancaster will be rewarded with a visit to the Maritime Museum, where the histories of the 18th-century transatlantic maritime trade of Lancaster, the Lancaster Canal and the fishing industry of Morecambe Bay are well illustrated (www.lancsmuseums.gov.uk). Take time to view Morecambe Bay or visit the Edwardian Butterfly House in Williamson Park (www.williamsonpark.com), or take a look at Lancaster Castle which dominates Castle Hill, above the River Lune. The Shire Hall contains a splendid display of heraldry (www.lancastercastle.com).

Gisburn Forest

Explore Lancashire's biggest forest and discover some of its flora and fauna.

Gisburn Forest

Gisburn Forest is Lancashire's biggest, covering 3,000 acres (1,215ha). It was opened in 1932, around the same time as Stocks Reservoir, alongside it. The reservoir is huge, formed by damming the River Hodder and submerging the village of Stocks in the process of providing drinking water for the towns of central Lancashire. When it's full it can hold 2.6 billion gallons. Gisburn Forest and Stocks Reservoir are favoured places for birdwatchers. In springtime, keep an eye open for visiting osprey, which quite often use the reservoir for on-the-wing food supplies on their way northwards to Scotland at breeding time.

You will almost certainly spot members of the tit family, notably great, blue and coal tits, and may be lucky to see a great-spotted woodpecker. This is a good time, too, to look for orchids: Gisburn is renowned for its common spotted orchid, which flourishes in the damp conditions.

the ride

1 Set off along a narrow path from the car park, to a sharp left-hand bend, then descend, before climbing gently to pass a barrier, and reach a **broad forest trail**. Turn right, and about 100 yards (110m) later, when the track forks, keep forward. Before reaching a group of buildings (**Stephen Park**), leave the broad trail and turn right at a waymark onto a very narrow path that follows the edge of an open area, and finally heads back towards the buildings.

1h00 · **6 MILES** · **9.7 KM** · **LEVEL 1 2 3**

2 On reaching **Stephen Park,** turn right on a broad trail, which immediately forks. Keep left, climbing gently, and then heading downhill. Continue following the main trail as it weaves its way through the forest to a **barrier** coming up to a T-junction, where the three main forest cycle trails divide. Here turn left, pursuing the **Purple Trail**.

3 Continue to the access to **Hesbert Hall Farm,** and there branch right, passing a barrier into a short stretch of dense woodland with a clearing ahead. Now make a long descent to cross a **stream,** beyond which the track rises to a T-junction, where the Red and Green route rejoin. Turn left.

Top: Picnic tables in Gisburn Forest
Below: A view from the Gisburn Forest Trail

MAP: OS Explorer OL41 Forest of Bowland and Ribblesdale
START/FINISH: Cocklet Hill car park; grid ref: SD746550
TRAILS/TRACKS: mainly broad forest trails, some narrow paths and stony, bumpy trails
LANDSCAPE: forest
PUBLIC TOILETS: none on route
TOURIST INFORMATION: Clitheroe, tel: 01200 425566
CYCLE HIRE: Pedal Power, Waddington Road, Clitheroe, Lancashire BB7 2HJ, tel: 01200 422066
THE PUB: The Hark to Bounty, Slaidburn
⚠ Maps are useless in Gisburn - follow the Purple Trail. Stony trails and overhanging vegetation

Getting to the start

Gisburn Forest is well signed across the surrounding countryside, but the start is best reached along the B6478 from Slaidburn (south west) or Long Preston (north east).

Why do this cycle ride?

Forests like Gisburn are known for mile after mile of conifers with scarcely a decent view. But at Gisburn, more and more broadleaved trees are being planted, and areas are being cleared to allow for good views. The trails in Gisburn are waymarked; this route follows the shortest, the Purple Trail. Maps can't keep up-to-date with what is happening on the ground, so waymark chasing is the best way.

Researched and written by: Terry Marsh

4 The broad trail eventually leads on, after winding through the forest, to another T-junction. Here, turn left, descending, and following a bumpy route that brings **Stocks Reservoir** into view. Eventually, just before reaching a road, turn left at a **waymark post** onto a narrow path through mixed woodland to reach the **road**, which now crosses an arm of the reservoir.

5 On the other side, leave the road by turning left up a steep and narrow path – you may have to dismount here. Follow this through **woodland**, steep in places, and finally emerge at a broad forest track at a bend. Keep left and then forward, and climb to another **barrier** giving on to a T-junction. Turn right, and 100yds (110m) later turn left, having now rejoined the outward route, which is retraced to the start.

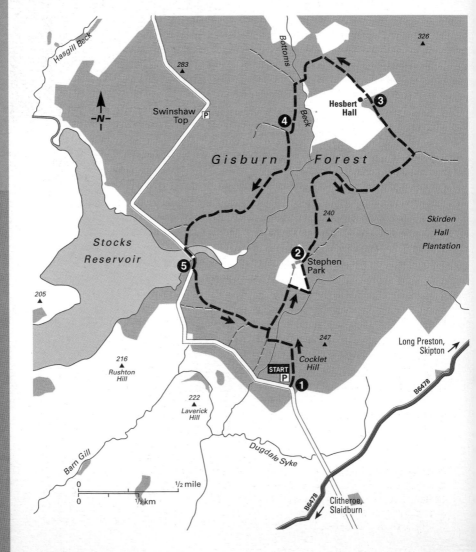

The Hark to Bounty

The setting – a beautiful village on the moors above Clitheroe – is one of the attractions of this historic stone pub. It dates from the 13th century and was known as the The Dog until 1875 when Bounty, the local squire's favourite hound, disturbed a post-inn drinking session with its loud baying. View the original first floor courtroom, for many years the main court between Lancaster and York, and still in use until 1937. It's now a function room, complete with old jury benches and a witness box. Downstairs, the atmospheric old bar has old-fashioned settles, exposed beams, a roaring log fire, plenty of brass ornaments and old pictures on the walls.

Food

Traditional favourites include home-made steak and kidney pie served with Theakston ale gravy, vegetable and cheese crumble, and grilled haddock topped with tomatoes and Lancashire cheese, supplemented by pasta and curries from the chalkboards. Snacks take in filled jacket potatoes and ploughman's lunches.

Family facilities

Children are very welcome throughout and there's a children's menu, high chairs, smaller portions and changing facilities.

Alternative refreshment stops

None on the route. Refreshments in Slaidburn and Clitheroe.

☞ Where to go from here

Developed on the site of former 17th-century cottages, Slaidburn Heritage Centre provides a site for exhibitions and information relating to the history of this fascinating area. South of Clitheroe are the 14th-century ruins of Whalley Abbey, originally a medieval monastery, set in the grounds of a 17th-century manor house, now a retreat and conference centre. Guided tours, visitor centre and coffee shop.

about the pub

The Hark to Bounty
Slaidburn, Clitheroe
Lancashire BB7 3EP
Tel: 01200 446246
www.harktobounty.co.uk

DIRECTIONS: from Gisburn Forest return to the B6478 and turn right for 3 miles (4.8km) to reach Slaidburn. Cross the river and take the second turning right for the pub

OPEN: daily; all day

FOOD: daily; all day Sunday

BREWERY/COMPANY: free house

REAL ALE: Pedigree, Theakston's Old Peculier, guest ales

ROOMS: 10 en suite

The Harland Way

Follow a picturesque railway line to discover Yorkshire's forgotten fortress.

Around Spofforth

Lying among the peaceful pastures of the Crimple Valley, Spofforth is an idyllic backwater for a Sunday afternoon ride. Go back in time to the medieval era and things were very different. A year after the Battle of Hastings, William the Conqueror's friend, William de Percy, made Spofforth his headquarters. The original dwelling would have been a fortified hall, of which nothing remains, but by the 13th century the castle was taking shape, built into the rock on which it stood. Subsequent alterations of the 14th and 15th centuries gave the castle its powerful walls and that strong Gothic look.

In 1309 Henry de Percy bought the Manor of Alnwick in Northumberland and made that his main residence, but the family's alliances were to land them in trouble on several occasions – after their rebellion against King Henry IV in 1408, and their support in the Wars of the Roses. On both occasions the Crown confiscated Spofforth Castle. The castle lay waste for around a hundred years until Henry, Lord Percy restored it in 1559. Within another hundred years, however, it was sacked

by Oliver Cromwell's forces during fierce fighting of the Civil War. Stand on the green today, and you can still feel the presence and imagine the times of turmoil endured by this rugged historic building.

the ride

1 With your back to the car park entrance, turn right along the railway trackbed, highlighted by a **Harland Way fingerpost**. The line has been exploded through the bedrock to reveal limestone crags, now hung with pleasant woodland that offers excellent shade on hot summer days.

2 Take the left fork at the junction that used to be known as the **Wetherby Triangle**. You're soon joined from the right by another branch of the line and together the routes head west towards Spofforth. Halfway along the track you have to dismount to get through a **metal gateway**, then again almost immediately at another gate. The trackbed forges through an avenue of beech, hawthorn, ash, and rowan before coming out into the open. Now you'll see thickets of wild roses and bramble, with scabious and purple vetch among the numerous wild flowers of the verges. There are wide views across cornfields, and soon the tower of **Spofforth church** comes into view ahead.

3 The Harland Way ends beyond a gate just short of the village. A gravel path veers right across a green on to **East Park Road**. This threads through **modern housing** to come to the main road where you should turn right. If you have young

The grounds of ruined Spofforth Castle

2h00 — **8 MILES** — **12.9 KM** — **LEVEL 1 2 3**

MAP: OS Explorer 289 Leeds
START/FINISH: Sicklinghall Road, Wetherby; grid ref: SE397483
TRAILS/TRACKS: well compacted gravel railway trackbed, lanes and smooth bridleways
LANDSCAPE: pastureland and village
PUBLIC TOILETS: none on route
TOURIST INFORMATION: Wetherby, tel: 01937 582151
CYCLE HIRE: none locally
THE PUB: The Castle, Spofforth
⚠ A short section of main road through Spofforth village

Getting to the start
From the A661 Wetherby to Harrogate road turn off on the westbound Sicklinghall Road then after 300yds (274m) a blue cycleway sign points to the car park on the right.

Why do this cycle ride?
The Harland Way forms the basis of a delightful rural ride following in the tracks of the steam trains and visiting one of Yorkshire's most fascinating Norman castles.

Researched and written by: John Gillham

Harland Way

NORTH YORKSHIRE

children it might be better to dismount to cross the road, and use the pavements to get to **The Castle** inn.

4 Just beyond the pub, where the road bends right, take the lane on the left, which heads for the **castle**. When you've seen the castle retrace your route past the pub then turn right along Park Road. Beyond the **houses** this becomes a stony bridleway, rising gently across the fields.

5 Ignore turn-offs until you come to **Fox Heads Farm**. Turn left along the track here, passing left of the farmhouse. The dirt and stone track descends to a bridge over a stream, then climbs again past an **old quarry**. Though there are a few climbs the track is still quite easy, being smooth-surfaced and fairly well drained. Often it's lined with bramble, ferns and foxgloves, with the odd tree. Just beyond

the summit of the hill the track bends right. After being joined from the right by another farm track it comes to the road, just to the west of **Sicklinghall village**.

6 Turn left along the road into the village. On the right there's a pond with lilies and coots, then on the left there's another pub, the **Scott Arms**. The winding road makes a long but gradual descent towards Wetherby, passing the upmarket **Linton Springs Hotel**. Beyond the hotel, ignore the right turn 'to Linton'. After passing through housing in the Wetherby suburbs watch out for the **blue cyclists' sign**. This marks the access road back to the car park.

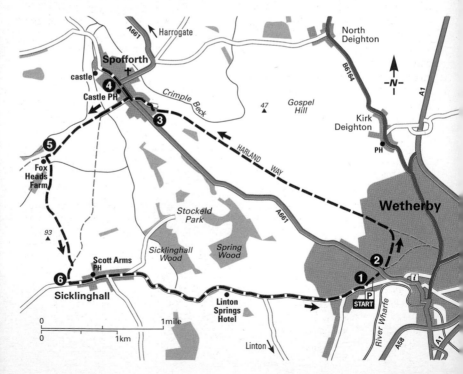

The Castle

Sited on Spofforth's main street, The Castle has old red sandstone walls clad with a little creeping ivy and, in summer, with colourful hanging baskets. There's a courtyard at the back for outdoor dining.

Food
The home-cooked traditional pub food includes ploughman's lunch, steaks, Sunday roasts, omelettes and pasta meals, alongside cod in beer batter, steak and kidney pie, Castle mixed grill and a range of vegetarian dishes.

Family facilities
Children are allowed in the eating areas of the bar. Smaller portions of any main course dishes on the menu are available.

Alternative refreshment stops
The Scott Arms at Sicklinghall.

☛ Where to go from here
The 58-acre (23.5ha) RHS Harlow Carr Botanical Gardens west of Harrogate includes a breathtaking streamside garden, peaceful woodland and arboretum, and a Museum of Gardening (www.rhs.org.uk). In Harrogate, the Royal Pump Room Museum tells the story of Harrogate's heyday as England's European spa (www.harrogate.gov.uk).

about the pub

The Castle
35 High Street, Spofforth
Harrogate, North Yorkshire HG3 1BQ
Tel: 01937 590200

DIRECTIONS: The Castle in Spofforth is on the route and lies on the corner at the top end of High Street, near the junction with Castle Street

PARKING: 24

OPEN: daily

FOOD: daily

BREWERY/COMPANY: Punch Taverns

REAL ALE: Black Sheep Bitter, Tetley's, John Smith's

Warter Wold

A pleasant countryside ride discovering the rolling Yorkshire Wolds and some charming villages.

The Yorkshire Wolds

The Yorkshire Wolds form the most northerly outcrop of chalk in Britain. Here, smooth, rounded hills top shallow valleys with streams trickling through grass and woodlands. Chalk makes rich fertile ground for farming and the prehistoric settlers did just that. In those days the hills were tree-covered, good for providing cover from wild animals, while the valleys were uninhabitable swamps. These settlers made clearings and left much evidence of their existence in the form of burial mounds (tumuli) and earthwork dykes – you'll see one of those from the bridleway south of Huggate.

The Romans conquered the region but settled quite peaceably here; you'll be riding along one of their roads into Warter. But the Normans were a little more brutal – William the Conqueror, angered by the resistance of the locals, set about his 'harrying of the North'. The whole area was sacked and set ablaze. Gone were the trees. The Wolds people never replanted them – some say it is because they believed it was possible that witches could hide behind them.

The Enclosure Acts of the late 1700s brought more significant changes. The large, straight-edged fields with long hawthorn hedges were set up then, allowing the patchwork of pasture and cornfields you see today. Villages like Warter and North Dalton had popped up in the valleys to be near the water table – look out for the dewponds and the water pumps.

the ride

1 From the car park, cycle back to the village green and turn right past the old **church**. Take the first right, a narrow road climbing steeply at first with a shallow grassy vale to the left.

2 There's a T-junction at the top of the hill, where you turn left signed '**Market Weighton & Dalton**', on the level, at first, then, beyond a left-hand bend, an easy descent. By a red-bricked house and a narrow wood turn right, highlighted by a **Middleton signpost**. After the first bend the road passes some high manicured hedges then beneath magnificent beech trees near **Middleton Lodge**.

3 The lane comes to a junction on the northern edge of **Middleton-on-the-Wolds**. Turn right if you want to have a look around then return to the same spot, or left past a **post box** and the last houses to continue the journey. From the top of the first hill there are fine views northwards across the rolling Wolds. There's a small

Looking across Warter Wold from the Bridleway

5h00 · **15 MILES** · **24 KM** · **LEVEL 123**

MAP: OS Explorer 294 Market Weighton & Yorkshire Wolds Central
START/FINISH: Warter village car park; grid ref: SE868502
TRAILS/TRACKS: country lanes, some hilly and an easy section of grass-track bridleway
LANDSCAPE: rolling hills
PUBLIC TOILETS: none on route
TOURIST INFORMATION: York, tel: 01904 621756
CYCLE HIRE: none locally
THE PUB: Wolds Inn, Huggate
ⓘ A long route with some hills. Not suitable for young children

Getting to the start
Leave the York ring road on the A1079, then at Barmby Moor take the Pocklington turn-off (B1246) to the left. Warter lies 5 miles (8km) along this road. Turn right at the village green to the signed village car park.

Why do this cycle ride?
If you want a good summer's day ride and would like to sample the Yorkshire Wolds without taking to mountain biking, this is your route.

Researched and written by: John Gillham

Warter Wold EAST YORKSHIRE

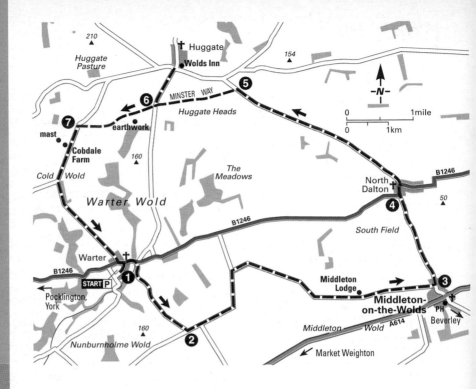

dip preceding a steady climb into Dalton village, where you meet the B road at the apex of a bend.

4 Go straight on towards the village centre where there's a splendid duck pond, then go left by the **Methodist chapel**. The road climbs steadily and is pleasant, with flower-decked verges.

5 After 3 miles (4.8km) turn left by a large **ash tree** on to a wide, rutted, grassy bridleway, part of the Minster Way. This firm track, lined by thorn bushes to the right and thistles to the left, eases across **Huggate Heads**. To the south the fields fall away into a shallow wooded vale. After 1.5 miles (2.4km) the bridleway comes to another lane.

6 Turn right to reach **Huggate**, and the **Wolds Inn**. Return along the lane to the

bridleway. This time turn right onto a similar grass track, which winds around hillsides above two steep-sided grassy vales that are so typical of the Yorkshire Wolds landscape.

7 Just beyond the second the track comes to the road. Climb left, past the communications mast and **Cobdale Farm**, then take the left fork, signed 'Warter'. It's the course of a Roman road, which, beyond **Lings Plantation**, makes a long steady descent. Brake gently here to control your speed. At the bottom of the hill lies **Warter** and an old building with a clock, dated 1868. Turn left here, then right at the green to pass a charming terrace of **whitewashed cottages** with thatched roofs and porches fronted by the quaint cast-iron street lamps from the Victorian era. The road leads back to the car park.

Wolds Inn

about the pub

Wolds Inn
Driffield Road, Huggate
Pocklington, East Yorkshire YO42 1YH
Tel: 01377 288217

DIRECTIONS: village signposted south off A166 between York and Driffield. Pub in village centre

PARKING: 45

OPEN: closed all day Monday and Friday lunch (except Bank Holidays)

FOOD: daily

BREWERY/COMPANY: free house

REAL ALE: Tetley, Timothy Taylor Landlord, summer guest beer

ROOMS: 3 en suite

Probably the highest inn on the Yorkshire Wolds, this venerable village local, close to the parish church, also claims 16th-century origins. Beneath a huddle of tiled roofs and white-painted chimneys, it sports an interior of wood panelling, gleaming brassware and open fires. Separate locals' games room and good real ale on tap. Pleasant rear garden with views of the surrounding Wolds. A great favourite with cyclists.

Food

Baguettes and sandwiches line up alongside bar main dishes of gammon and egg, home-made steak pie, grilled fillet of plaice, pork chops and mushrooms, and a weekly changing curry. A typical restaurant meal may feature cod and pancetta fishcakes followed by rack of lamb cooked in garlic, or decent steaks with all the trimmings. Sunday roast lunches.

Family facilities

Children are very welcome inside the pub. There's a children's menu, smaller portions of adult dishes are also available, notably good-value Sunday lunches, and there are high chairs.

Alternative refreshment stops

The Star Inn at North Dalton.

☛ Where to go from here

Head off to see Burnby Hall Gardens and Stuart Collection in Pocklington, where there are 9 acres (3.6ha) of beautiful gardens with lakes, woodland walks and a Victorian garden to explore. In Beverley, the Museum of Army Transport tells the story of army transport from horse-drawn wagons to the present.

Goosnargh and Beacon Fell Country Park

Ride the lanes of Lancashire to the top of richly wooded Beacon Fell.

Sculpture Trail

From the Visitor Centre on Beacon Fell there is a Sculpture Trail featuring the work of local artist Thompson Dagnall, which uses materials found locally. Along the way you might find a serpent and, near the top of the fell, a bat hidden in the trees. All these are wooden, of course, but the country park is a remarkable habitat, and you should keep eyes and ears open for chaffinch, willow warbler, goldcrest, bullfinch, siskin and the occasional crossbill. Rabbits and hares are plentiful, too, and easily spotted in the bushes and the surrounding farm fields. Not surprisingly, they tend to be timid, as the sky here is patrolled by kestrels, sparrowhawk and tawny owls on the lookout for a ready meal, and stoat, weasel and fox are not above a rabbit lunch.

The breathtaking view from Beacon Fell across the Bowland Fells

the ride

1 Begin past **Bushell House** and immediately turn left into **Mill Lane**, a narrow lane flanked by hedgerows, climbing gently, and continuing past houses out into a more rural setting, and later descending through a dip to cross a bridge. Go past the end of **Broadith Lane**, and keep forward passing Curwen Lane, and remaining on Mill Lane to pass through a tunnel of trees to a crossroads.

2 Keep forward into **Syke House Lane**, with Beacon Fell soon coming into view. Stay on the main road, passing Church Lane and Bullsnape Lane and, just after passing **Back Lane**, descend gently through bends into a dip and out through a lightly wooded stretch. Turn left for **Beacon Fell Country Park**, into Barns Lane.

3 When the road makes a pronounced right-hand bend, go left into **Carwags Lane**, leaving the main road for a very

Looking back towards Beacon Fell

3h00	14 MILES	22 KM	LEVEL 123

MAP: OS Explorer 286 Blackpool and Preston and OL41 Forest of Bowland and Ribblesdale

START/FINISH: Public parking adjacent to the church in Goosnargh; grid ref: SD559369

TRAILS/TRACKS: entirely on country lanes, some very narrow with high hedgerows

LANDSCAPE: rolling farmland

PUBLIC TOILETS: none on route

TOURIST INFORMATION: Clitheroe, tel: 01200 425566

CYCLE HIRE: Pedal Power, Waddington Road, Clitheroe, Lancashire BB7 2HJ, tel: 01200 422066

THE PUB: Bushells Arms, Goosnargh

🛈 There is a very long but steady ascent up to Beacon Fell and around its circular route, followed by equally long and steady descents

Getting to the start

Goosnargh lies about 5 miles (8km) north east of Preston, and is easily reached via M6 (Jct 32) and M55 (Jct 1), north on A6 to Broughton, and then right to Goosnargh. At the post office, turn left into Church Lane, and follow this north to the start.

Why do this cycle ride?

Beacon Fell Country Park is an isolated hill rising to 873ft (266m), on the edge of the Bowland Fells. It is an area of rough moorland and woodland within the Forest of Bowland Area of Outstanding Natural Beauty, and was one of the first designated country parks in Britain. There are tremendous views north and south from the highest ground, and the approach along country lanes displays rural Lancashire at its very best.

Researched and written by: Terry Marsh

narrow lane, and a very long and steady climb, which young children may find tiring, up towards Beacon Fell. On reaching **Beacon Fell Road**, go forward into a one-way system.

4 At the turning to **Crombleholme Fold** you need to make a decision. The circuit around Beacon Fell is delightful, but one-way: Crombleholme Fold is the continuing route, but a short way beyond the junction lies the **Bowland Visitor Centre**, toilets, café and information point. Once you pass Crombleholme Fold, you are committed to cycling all the way around the fell, with still more ascent on the northern side. Cycling within the woodland is permitted, but only on surfaced tracks. If you go around the fell – recommended – you will be treated to lovely views northwards to the **Bowland Fells**, and in due course return to the Crombleholme Fold turning. Turn left, descending steeply. At a T-junction, turn left into **Bleasdale Road**, and shortly left again into **Button Street**.

5 Follow a hedgerowed lane into the village of **Inglewhite**. Go past the village green to a crossroads, and keep forward into **Silk Mill Lane**, which gradually descends to cross **Sparting Brook**, climbing steadily on the other side. At a T-junction, turn right onto **Langley Lane** (signed for Preston).

6 Go through two S-bends, followed by a long, more or less straight and level section to a pronounced left bend (occasional flooding here), that leads down to a **hump bridge**, and a short climb beyond. Continue as far as **Goosnargh Lane**, and there turn left to return to **Goosnargh village**.

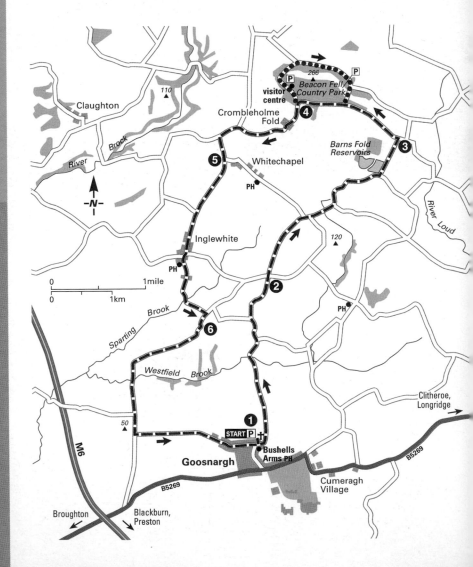

Bushells Arms

Dr Bushell was a philanthropic Georgian who built his villagers not just a hospital, but this pub too. And he chose a lovely spot, beside the village green and overlooking the parish church. Expect a congenial and relaxing atmosphere in the cosy beamed bar, where you will find leather armchairs and a log fire in the stone fireplace. There's also an intimate candlelit restaurant.

Food

For a light bite you could peruse the new Mediterranean tapas menu, which lists dishes such as Madeira chicken and roasted vegetables. For something more substantial tuck into beer battered cod, the Bushell burger with pepper sauce and hand-cut chips, or the renowned roasted Goosnargh duckling with apple sauce.

Family facilities

Families are welcome and smaller portions from the main menu can be provided for children. Make use of the secluded rear garden on fine days, replete with flower borders and a spacious lawn.

Alternative refreshment stops

Café, picnic and barbecue sites in the country park, plus pubs in Goosnargh.

☛ Where to go from here

Visit the ancient market town of Clitheroe and explore the town's 12th-century castle. The Castle Museum brings to life the history and geology of the Ribble Valley. At the National Football Museum in Preston you can take a fascinating trip through football past and present. There's a fine display of memorabilia, interactive displays that allow visitors to commentate on football matches, and virtual trips to every League ground in the country (www.nationalfootballmuseum.com).

about the pub

Bushells Arms
Church Lane, Goosnargh
Preston, Lancashire PR3 2BH
Tel: 01772 865235

DIRECTIONS: see Getting to the start
PARKING: use public car park opposite
OPEN: all day; closed Monday except Bank Holidays
FOOD: daily
BREWERY/COMPANY: Enterprise Inns
REAL ALE: Marston's Pedigree, Timothy Taylor Landlord, Black Sheep Bitter, Tetley, guest beers

Foulridge to Greenber Field

An easy ride along the
Leeds to Liverpool Canal,
and a chance encounter
with stalactites and a ghost.

Above and below the ground
Kingfishers are known to dart about along
the canal, so it is worth keeping an eye
open for these arrows of iridescence. They
like to perch on branches overhanging the
canal, from which they dive into the water
to catch small fish.

Well worth a visit are the cellars of the
Anchor Inn at Salterforth, which have an
impressive array of 'straw' stalactites, and
some rather stunted stalagmites. It's
certainly not what you expect; nor is the

flooded cellar; nor is the story of Joseph
Widdup, who hanged himself in the cellar,
and whose ghost still haunts the pub. Don't
worry, he's not a fearsome spirit, just rather
playful, as the barstaff may well tell you.

the ride

1 This ride simply follows the **canal** to the
locks at Greenber Field, and then comes
back again. The towpath gives elevated
views of the surrounding countryside, and
encounters no hindrance until a gate
complex is reached just past **The Anchor
Inn** at Salterforth.

2 Continue as far as **Bridge No. 153**, and
there, with care, emerge briefly onto

Riding along the towpath of the Leeds and Liverpool Canal at Greenber Field

1h30	8.25 MILES	13.2 KM	LEVEL 123

MAP: OS Explorer OL21 South Pennies

START/FINISH: Foulridge Wharf; grid ref: SD888427

TRAILS/TRACKS: good towpath, with just a few cobbles in places

LANDSCAPE: mainly farmland, with rolling hills in the distance and little urbanisation

PUBLIC TOILETS: none on route

TOURIST INFORMATION: Barnoldswick (Colne), tel: 01282 666704

CYCLE HIRE: Pedal Power, Waddington Road, Clitheroe, Lancashire BB7 2HJ, tel: 01200 422066

THE PUB: The Anchor Inn, Salterforth

🛇 Care to be taken as whole ride is beside the canal

Getting to the start

Foulridge lies just over 1 mile (1.6km) north of Colne along the A56 to Skipton. In the centre of Foulridge, take the B6251, and follow signs for Foulridge Wharf. There is a small car park at the wharf.

Why do this cycle ride?

This is Pendle, a delightful mix of witchcraft and enchanting scenery, a place of ancient market towns and stone-built villages. But it so much more; bordering Yorkshire, there are extensive views framed by trees alongside the canal, and a pastoral loveliness. The ride is entirely flat all the way, and with only one brief road crossing to deal with as you switch sides of the canal, the miles simply slip by.

Researched and written by: Terry Marsh

a minor road in order to switch sides of the canal. Press on, passing some **light industrial units,** with an increasing amount of urbanisation as the route passes through the suburbs of **Barnoldswick**. This is short-lived, and soon farmland landscapes return, as the towpath heads for the locks at **Greenber Field**, once voted the best-kept locks in Britain.

3 The return route simply meanders back along the easygoing canal **towpath,** but the ride can be pleasantly extended by perhaps calling in for a drink at The Anchor Inn on the homeward stretch.

Foulridge

LANCASHIRE

Cyclists share the towpath of the Leeds and Liverpool Canal with walkers

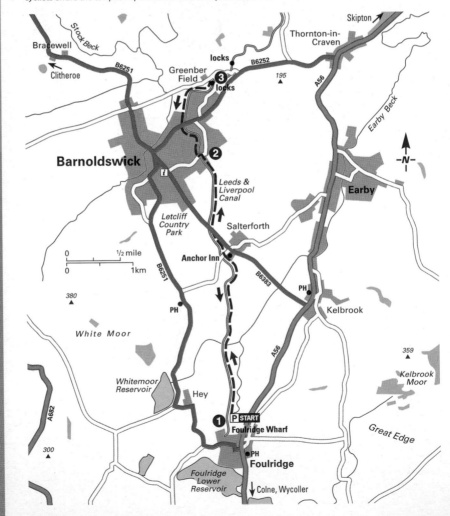

Foulridge LANCASHIRE

The Anchor Inn

This friendly, homely and welcoming inn, together with the barn known as 'The Rough' at the rear, are amongst the oldest buildings in Salterforth, believed to date back to around 1655. It was the old 'travellers' rest', built on an old packhorse way, a salt road from Cheshire to Yorkshire. When the adjacent Leeds and Liverpool Canal was excavated between 1770 and 1816, the building became damp, so a new inn was erected, with the travellers' rest as the cellar. Today, there are four small, beamed rooms, and cellars that hold a fabulous stalactite formation, as well as a resident ghost, Joseph Widdup, whose family lived at the inn – he hanged himself in the cellar.

Food

Generous portions of traditional pub food range from basic snacks and Yorkshire puddings with various fillings to steak and kidney pie, gammon topped with onions and Wensleydale cheese, and lamb curries.

Family facilities

The pub is a great stop-off point on the route, especially for children as there's a play area in the canalside garden. A genuine welcome awaits inside the pub if the weather is poor. Young children have their own menu.

Alternative refreshment stops

Foulridge Tea Rooms serves hot meals and snacks and freshly baked cakes.

☛ Where to go from here

Wycoller Country Park at Trawden is renowned for its association with the Brontë sisters. There's a ruined 16th-century hall, a craft centre and tea room. Housed in the old Grammar School at Earby, the Museum of Yorkshire Dales Lead Mining contains a comprehensive collection of historical mining artefacts. Head east to Skipton and visit England's most complete medieval castle (www.skiptoncastle.co.uk).

about the pub

The Anchor Inn
Salterforth Lane, Salterforth
Barnoldswick, Lancashire BB18 5TT
Tel: 01282 813186

DIRECTIONS: beside the canal at Salterforth Bridge, off the B6383 between the A56 at Kelbrook and Barnoldswick

PARKING: 40

OPEN: daily; all day

FOOD: daily; all day Saturday and Sunday

BREWERY/COMPANY: Scottish & Newcastle

REAL ALE: John Smiths Cask, Courage Directors, Theakston's Best, guest beers

Foulridge LANCASHIRE

From Esholt to the Five Rise Locks

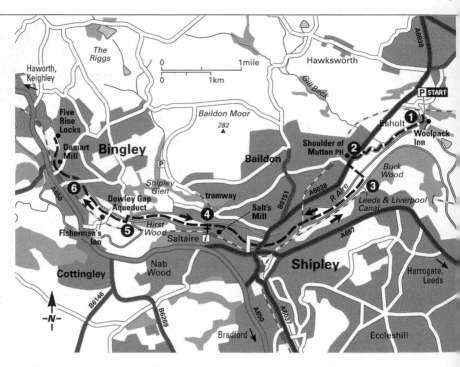

A slice of West Yorkshire from the rural environs of the TV series to the canalside mill towns of the Aire Valley.

Saltaire

Though the Industrial Revolution brought prosperity to the ruling classes, it brought great inequalities elsewhere. While the factory owners lived in their mansions in the country, their workers tended to live in overcrowded and unhygienic city streets. Wealthy Bradford mill owner Sir Titus Salt had been dismayed by this situation. He decided to move his mills into one unit, which would be built in a cleaner

environment and would be part of a newly constructed model village. After finding his site at Shipley in the Aire Valley, Salt employed the best architects to design his project – Saltaire.

The village comprised 22 streets, all named after Salt's family members, and, on its completion in 1876, there were over 800 beautifully constructed houses in an area of 25 acres (10ha). Particularly notable are the beautiful Venetian-style Congregational church and the six-storey mill. The mill closed down in 1892, following a deep recession, and Saltaire lay idle and degenerating. However, almost a hundred years later a Leeds millionaire, Jonathan Silver, restored the mill, which now houses

1h45 — **7 MILES** — **11.3 KM** — **LEVEL 123**

the 1853 Gallery with hundreds of exhibits by local artist David Hockney. The village has been brought to life again with restaurants, a pub, antiques dealers and organised boat trips along the canal.

the ride

1 Turn left out of the car park on to the road (with care) and descend to the village. **The Woolpack,** post office and row of cottages, as featured for many years on the TV series *Emmerdale*, are on the left. Continue down the lane, passing the **Esholt Sports Club** and the campsite. The terraces of Bunker Hill on the right were *Emmerdale*'s Demdyke Row. Over a stone bridge and past a driving range the lane draws alongside the River Aire, then climbs right to meet the A6038 opposite the **Shoulder of Mutton pub**. It would be best to dismount here.

2 Turn left, following the footpath, then left again down **Buck Lane**. Shortly take the right fork, a mud and stone scrub-lined track that descends to the River Aire. Here a **steel bridge** built in 1889 leads to the far bank, where the track climbs to reach the Leeds–Liverpool Canal at **Buck Wood**.

A visitors' farm at Esholt

MAP: OS Explorer 288 Bradford and Huddersfield
START/FINISH: Esholt; grid ref: SE182404
TRAILS/TRACKS: all quiet country lanes and towpath
LANDSCAPE: semi-rural and urban
PUBLIC TOILETS: Esholt car park and Five Rise Locks
TOURIST INFORMATION: Saltaire, tel: 01274 774993
CYCLE HIRE: none locally
THE PUB: The Fisherman's Inn, Bingley
🛈 Busy road (A6038) at point 2; a steepish descent along the Buck Lane track to the river (point 2). Take extra care along the canal towpath

Getting to the start
Esholt lies on the north bank of the River Aire to the north east of Bradford. Follow the A650 trunk road to Shipley, then the A6038 through Baildon, before turning right for Esholt. The car park is on the hill, just to the north of the town and near the railway viaduct.

Why do this cycle ride?
This cycle ride visits some of the wonders of the Industrial Revolution, including Titus Salt's model village and the Bingley Five Rise Locks.

Researched and written by: John Gillham

Aire Valley WEST YORKSHIRE

73

3 Turn right along the **towpath** here. After about 100yds (91m) you'll come across a **bench**, which some kind soul has sited right next to bushes that will in late August be endowed with some of the most luscious blackberries. We had a feast! The towpath is firm and wide at first, but beyond **bridge 209a**, carrying the railway to Baildon, it narrows considerably. If there are a lot of walkers about it would be best to follow the adjacent tarred lane and rejoin the towpath beyond the next bridge (209). Note: whichever way you choose, you'll be crossing traffic at this second bridge. At this point the canal is cutting through the industrial outskirts of Shipley, but soon things improve. Some smart **mill buildings** and a tower appear. You're entering the model mill town of Saltaire. Spend some time here; it's a fascinating place.

4 The towpath continues along a pleasing tree-lined section of the canal. Peeping through boughs on the left you'll see **Titus Salt's church**. At **Hirst Wood** beyond Saltaire, the River Aire and the canal draw

close and the towpath continues on a narrow stretch of land between the two.

5 The canal finally crosses the river along the **Dowley Gap Aqueduct**. At bridge 206 the towpath on this side of the canal ends. Ride up the ramp, cross over the ridge, then descend to the towpath along the other side. At the next bridge **The Fisherman's Inn** has a beer garden.

6 The final stretch of the canal takes you through Bingley. There have been many changes here for the building of the Bingley Relief Road. After passing the huge **Damart Mill** and the three-rise staircase locks, you come to another tree-lined section before arriving at Bingley's famous **Five Rise Locks**. There's a steep but short climb to the top, but your reward is the fine view back to Bingley's woollen mills and chimneys and the chance of more refreshment at the lockside café. Retrace your route back along the canal to Esholt.

Five Rise Locks at Bingley

The Fisherman's Inn

This understated stone-built pub is conveniently sited right by the canal banks close to Bingley's famous Five Rise Locks. In summer there is a large attractive beer garden with wheelchair access and with pleasing views to the canal and across the Aire Valley. Very good standard of food, with a blackboard full of specials.

Food

Bar meals range from snacks and light bites to home-made pie of the day and sizzling steaks. There is a range of salads (chicken Caesar salad), ploughman's lunches, hot and cold sandwiches, filled jacket potatoes, gammon steak, and daily specials featuring fresh fish.

Family facilities

The pub has a children's certificate so they are very welcome throughout. There's a children's menu and smaller portions of main menu dishes are available.

Alternative refreshment stops

Before or after the ride you could try the Woolpack Inn at Esholt or, in Saltaire, there's Fanny's Café. In Bingley, there's the Five Rise Locks Café and Store.

☞ Where to go from here

You could take a walk along the signposted route from Saltaire to Shipley Glen, a popular picnic spot with a visitor centre and tramway up the hillside. For more information about the model mill town of Saltaire visit www.saltaire.yorks.com. Take a trip on the Keighley and Worth Valley Railway through the heart of Brontë country as it climbs to Haworth en route to Oxenhope. There are locomotive workshops at Haworth and an award-winning museum at Ingrow West (www.kwvr.co.uk).

about the pub

The Fisherman's Inn
Wagon Lane, Dowley Gap,
Bingley, West Yorkshire BD16 1TB
Tel: 01274 561697

DIRECTIONS: follow the A650 through Shipley. Just beyond where this crosses the River Aire at Cottingley, turn right along Wagon Lane towards Dowley Gap. The pub is on the right beyond the bridge over the railway

PARKING: 20

OPEN: daily; all day

FOOD: daily

BREWERY/COMPANY: Enterprise Inns

REAL ALE: guest beers

York's solar cycle path

A railway track cycle ride with space in mind as well as a visit to one of England's most historic cities.

The railway

York is a railway city so what better way to approach it than on an old railway line? And this old railway line was a famous one – part of the London King's Cross to Edinburgh East Coast Line. Here the *Flying Scotsman* and the world's fastest steam engine, the *Mallard*, thundered along the tracks carrying long trains of dark-red carriages.

So why did they close this stretch? Well, in the early 1980s an ultramodern coalfield at Selby was developed, necessitating a diversion of the railway to avoid the risk of subsidence. Sustrans bought the old line and set about their first major project – a new cycle track, from Riccall to York.

For budding astronomers the line includes a 6.4-mile (10km) scale model of the Solar System, with the Sun being closest to York and Pluto sited near Riccall. Perhaps one of the most fascinating aspects is the Naburn Swing Bridge spanning the River Ouse. Sad and dowdy, its old grey metal structure is showing its age, but there's a fascinating sculpture set across the top. 'The Fisher of Dreams' by Pete Rogers shows an angler sitting peacefully astride the bridge-top with his faithful dog. As you pass below, look closer at that naughty hound, for he is waiting to pee on your bike.

the ride

1 Follow the narrow dirt path leading down to the main trackbed where you turn right. The cycling is easy on a fairly level firm surface. After passing beneath the bridge at **Maude Ridding** and **Naburn Wood** you come to the first planet en route – Uranus. The **church spire** you can see at ten to the hour is that of Naburn village, and soon you pass under the bridge carrying Moor Lane, the Naburn road. Some woods largely obscure the village as you get closer but if you want to visit the village it can be accessed on the left by the **Howden Bridge**, where you see the ringed Saturn model.

2 Just a short way further along the track you reach **Naburn Bridge,** a huge steel structure that carries the track over the River Ouse and its marina. The bridge looks a little neglected, except for the **sculptures** topping it (see 'The Railway'), but it does offer fine views of the tree-lined Ouse, its boats and the vast plains of York. Over the bridge the track continues into the suburb of **Bishopsthorpe** where planet Jupiter awaits.

3 Suddenly there's a sign saying end of the railway track and you find yourself on a **housing estate** without having seen Earth. Don't worry – follow the blue and white cycleway signs first to the right, then left, and you'll soon be back on a tarred track passing Mars, Earth, Venus and Mercury in quick succession.

4 The track passes under the **York Ring Road**. On the other side there's a huge golden globe representing the Sun. Here

Wheeling along the York–Selby cycle track

4h00 — **14 MILES** — **22.6 KM** — **LEVEL 1**23

the path splits. This is a logical finishing point for those with young children, who will retrace their route back to Escrick. Otherwise, turn right following the tarred track running parallel to the ring road before skirting several fields. The main stand of **York Racecourse** comes into view and the path rounds it to the right, crossing two straights before turning left towards the right side of the **stand**.

5 The path comes to a road just south of the famous **Terry's chocolate factory**, which shut down in September 2005. Cross the road at the nearby crossing, turn left along the cycle/walkway, then right on a tarred track descending to the banks of the River Ouse. Turn left along the **riverside promenade**. You'll soon see the ultramodern **Millennium Bridge**. Past **Rowntree Park** and a campsite you follow a quiet back street, Terry Avenue, which still follows the riverside towards the centre of York. Now you'll see the large red and white **pleasure boats** cruising the river.

6 A block of buildings now separates the road from the river. Shortly, at the **Cock and Bottle pub**, turn right back to the riverside, where you should turn left. There are some **cycle racks** by the Ouse Bridge. On the opposite side of the river you'll see the whitewashed **Kings Arms**. To get to it just climb the steps ahead, turn right over the bridge and down the other side; or you could look around the city first: The Railway Museum, the Minster and the Shambles are a must. Retrace your route back along the railway path to Escrick.

MAP: OS Explorer 290 York
START/FINISH: Escrick; grid ref: SE616419
TRAILS/TRACKS: easy-riding former rail track plus back roads
LANDSCAPE: field, suburb and city
PUBLIC TOILETS: none on route
TOURIST INFORMATION: York, tel: 01904 621756
CYCLE HIRE: Europcar Cycle Hire, Platform 1, York Station, tel: 01904 656161
THE PUB: Kings Arms, Kings Staithe, York
🛈 The route crosses a road and mixes with light traffic from Point 5 (the old Terry's factory) to the centre of York

Getting to the start
Escrick is just off the A19, 7 miles (11.3km) south east of York. From the north take the A19 turn-off from the A64 ring road, then half a mile (800m) beyond Escrick take the first turn on the right. Turn left at the nearside of the brick-built railway bridge following a rough stone track down to the car park. From the south follow the A19 to York (junction 34 from the M62) and turn left just short of Escrick.

Why do this cycle ride?
If you're new to cycling this is one of the easier routes with smooth surfaces and little traffic, even in the centre of York. The railway verges are flower-filled in spring and summer and the views are superb for most of the way.

Researched and written by: John Gillham

York

NORTH YORKSHIRE

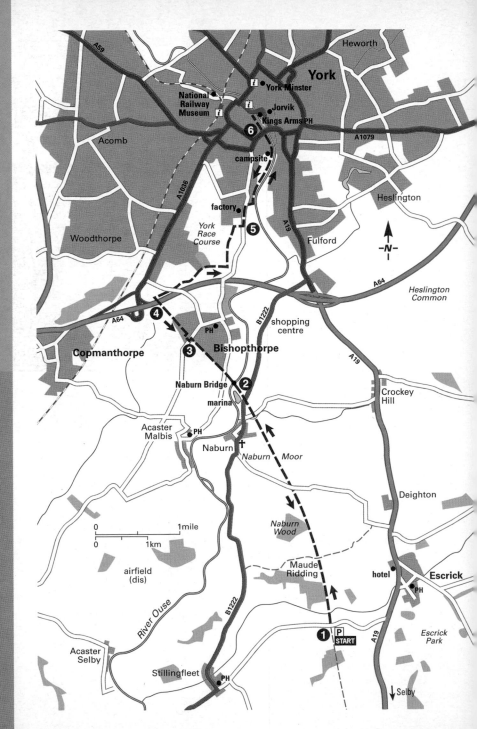

York NORTH YORKSHIRE

Kings Arms

York's most famous pub is sited right by the river. Each time the Ouse bursts its banks TV cameramen flock to the Kings Arms to capture the floodwaters flowing through the bar – there's a marker by the door that shows the level of famous floods of the past. For that reason, the pub's interior furnishings are spartan. It's a joy, however, to dine on their outside tables, which are laid across a cobbled area, right by the river. The food is simple, but oh-so-tasty alfresco style!

Food
The traditional pub food served here comes in the form of home-made steak pie, a daily roast, and changing chalkboard specials.

Family facilities
Young children are not allowed inside the pub. The cobbled riverside area offers a most attractive venue for alfresco dining but children need to be supervised at all times.

Alternative refreshment stops
Though there's nothing en route, there's an extremely wide choice of cafés and pubs in the centre of the city.

☞ Where to go from here
While you're in York a visit to the fine minster is a must, as is Jorvik (www.vikingjorvik.com) where you discover what life was like in Viking-age Yorkshire. At the National Railway Museum (www.nrm.org.uk), you will see trains that steamed along the track you've just been on, including the pale-blue streamlined Mallard.

York

NORTH YORKSHIRE

about the pub

Kings Arms
Kings Staithe, York,
North Yorkshire Yo1 9SN
Tel 01904 659435

DIRECTIONS: Kings Staithe is on the opposite bank of the river to the ride's finishing point
PARKING: none
OPEN: daily; all day
FOOD: no food in the evenings
BREWERY/COMPANY: Samuel Smiths
REAL ALE: none

Wheels through the Wolds

Gentle riding through rich, rolling farmland.

The Hudson Way

The route takes its name from George Hudson (1800–71), originally from Howsham, about 20 miles (32km) away, who became known as the 'Railway King'. Hudson was a financier (and sometimes a less than scrupulous one) rather than an engineer, who masterminded many of the great railway projects in the boom years of the middle 19th century. The line from York,

via Market Weighton to Beverley, was a relatively small part of his empire.

There are abundant opportunities for wildlife-spotting all along the railway route, but Kiplingcotes Chalk Pit is of particular interest. First worked in the 1860s to provide chalk for the railway, the pit closed in 1902 and is now managed as a Nature Reserve by Yorkshire Wildlife Trust. It features several distinct habitats: the quarry floor, the steep chalk faces, and the original grassland above, making it home to a wide variety of wild flowers. These in turn support a great range of butterflies, at their best in July, when more than 20 species may be seen.

Cycling out of South Dalton

Among the various crops farmed locally, one of the most distinctive yet least familiar is borage. At a distance you may think that the purple-blue fields are growing lavender but at closer range the two plants are quite different. Borage is a sturdy plant, which produces star-shaped flowers. The young leaves were traditionally used in salads and the flowers are also edible, but it is principally grown as a source of oil, and has many uses in aromatherapy and herbal medicine; ancient wisdom has it that it will cheer you up and give you courage. It is not recommended to handle borage plants without gloves as they are covered in stiff, prickly hairs.

the ride

1 With your back to the road, turn right along the **railway track**. The actual riding surface is quite narrow, flanked by lush grass and then flowery banks, with lots of willowherb and scabious. Soon pass an access gate for **Kiplingcotes Chalk Pit** (the crumbling chalk faces can be seen by simply continuing along the track). Dip down through staggered barriers to cross a farm track where a bridge is missing, and up the other side to resume. The track soon leads out into a car park at the former Kiplingcotes station. There is an information board here and the **old signal box** is sometimes open as an information centre.

2 Keep straight on past the old platforms. Negotiate another set of barriers and dip, and shortly after cross the tarmac lane to **Wold Farm**. The views open out briefly but then it's back into a cutting – watch out for nettles and brambles. Go up a slight rise

| 2h00 | 10.75 MILES | 17.3 KM | LEVEL 1 2 3 |

SHORTER ALTERNATIVE ROUTE

| 1h30 | 10 MILES | 16.1 KM | LEVEL 1 2 3 |

MAP: OS Explorer 294 Market Weighton and Yorkshire Wolds Central

START/FINISH: Car park near Kiplingcotes Chalk Pit; grid ref: SE909430

TRAILS/TRACKS: Old railway track, narrow in places; optional return on lanes

LANDSCAPE: rolling farmland with scattered woods

PUBLIC TOILETS: none on route

TOURIST INFORMATION: Beverley, tel: 01482 867430

CYCLE HIRE: none locally

THE PUB: Light Dragoon, Etton

Getting to the start

Follow A1079 east from York, skirt round Market Weighton and climb up on to the Wolds. Turn left at the first crossroads and follow the road down to a junction just before a bridge. Turn left then go for about 1.25 miles (2km) to a small car park on the right.

Why do this cycle ride?

To many people a rolling landscape of chalk hills, covered in broad fields and scattered woods, is quintessentially English. The Yorkshire Wolds produces gentle scenery, most of it given over to farming. The route follows the trackbed of a former railway line, which can be followed for the full distance of 11 or so miles (about 18km) from Market Weighton to Beverley. Those who want to avoid road riding entirely can ride it as an out-and-back route, but the suggested return through the lanes is very pleasant.

Researched and written by: Jon Sparks

The Wolds EAST YORKSHIRE

to cross a lane and dip back down on to the **railway track**. Continue until it becomes necessary to drop down right, quite steeply, to a lane.

3 Cross and climb back up the other side on to the embankment. Soon there's a view ahead towards the village of Etton. Cross the track to **Etton Fields Farm**, and another field track shortly after. The following section can be quite muddy. (Those who are planning an out-and-back ride could turn round before the muddy section.) Where the shrouding trees fall back and the surroundings open out, look out for the stump of a **windmill** on the left. Just before a bridge over the track ahead, go right up a narrower track to a road.

4 Turn left, go over the bridge and follow the road straight down into the village of **Etton**. At the T-junction turn left. **The Light Dragoon** is almost opposite.

5 Continue along the village street. Just after the **last houses** turn right, signposted for South Dalton, and up a short climb. Dead ahead as the gradient eases is the tall prominent spire of **St Mary's Church**, South Dalton. As the road begins to descend, turn left at a crossroads, signposted to Kiplingcotes and Market Weighton.

6 The road rolls along the crest of a broad ridge before a steeper descent leads down to an **angled crossroads**. Go left, signposted for Market Weighton, Kiplingcotes station and the Hudson Way. Just after passing a right turn to **Middleton-on-the-Wold**, turn left up the tarmac track that leads to Kiplingcotes station. Bear right back along the **railway track** to the start.

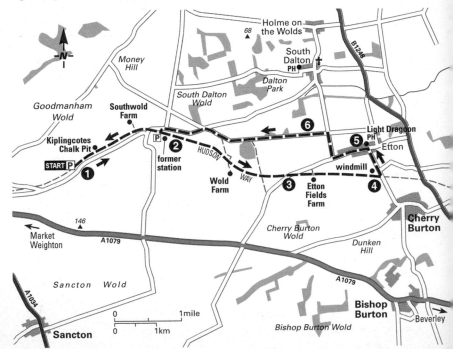

The Wolds EAST YORKSHIRE

The Light Dragoon

is more extensive and may include Etton salad (black pudding, bacon and feta cheese), home-made steak pie with shortcrust pastry top, lasagne and prime steaks with sauces.

Family facilities

Children are made very welcome here. Youngsters have their own menu and some play equipment in the garden.

Alternative refreshment stops

None on route. Options in Cherry Burton.

☞ Where to go from here

Beverley and Market Weighton are both historic market towns and well worth exploring on foot. Visit the impressive Minster and enjoy a drink in the utterly unspoilt and candlelit White Horse Inn (Nellies) in Beverley.

Even if you don't plan on making the return through the lanes, it's not a problem to include this fine pub in your ride, as it's only about 0.5 mile (800m) from the nearest point on the railway track. It sits firmly at the centre of the charming village of Etton, which is not much more than one long street. The lounge bar is cosy and comfortable and some old wagon wheels incorporated into partitions are a notable feature. There's a separate dining room behind, housed in a modern extension that harmonises reasonably well with the original building. There's also a very pleasant garden, well away from road and car park, with swings and slide for the youngsters. On a summer evening the sky can be alive with swifts and swallows.

Food

At lunchtime tuck into various sandwiches, salads, pies and steak. The evening menu

about the pub

The Light Dragoon
Main Street, Etton
Beverley, East Yorkshire HU17 7PQ
Tel: 01430 810282

DIRECTIONS: Etton is located 1 mile (1.6km) off the B1248 north west of Beverley. Pub is on the right in the village centre opposite a road junction

PARKING: 30

OPEN: daily

FOOD: daily

BREWERY/COMPANY: Scottish & Newcastle

REAL ALE: Black Bull

The Wolds **EAST YORKSHIRE**

Cuerden Valley to Preston and back

Discover Chorley's best-kept
secret – the valley of the
River Lostock.

Flora & fauna

Most of Cuerden's 700 acres (284ha) are
actively farmed, providing changing scenes
throughout the year. The Valley Park is
home to foxes, grey squirrels, great-spotted
and green woodpeckers, patrolling
buzzards and the occasional sparrowhawk,
as well as a host of smaller birds, up to 70
species in all. The Preston Junction Nature
Reserve, north of Bamber Bridge, is a good
place to spot butterflies – common blue,
small copper, meadow brown, wall brown,

gatekeeper, orange tip, small tortoiseshell.
There are also some attractive ponds along
this stretch, bright in spring and summer
with yellow waterlilies. The reserve was
built around the trackbed of the old
Preston tramway.

Cuerden Hall is owned by the Sue Ryder
Foundation and houses a small cafeteria; it
is off-route, but easily accessible by turning
left on reaching the A49 (rather than the
route continuation, which goes right).

the ride

1 Leave the car park and immediately
turn left onto the **Cuerden Valley Cycle
Route**. At a junction bear left onto a slightly
narrower track, and continue onto a
surfaced track, climbing a little and then
going forward to meet a main road. Turn
right for 120 yards (100m), and then turn
left to rejoin the cycle route.

2 The route through the valley park
follows a broad, clear track, at one
point bending right and left to pass through
the edge of woodland before rejoining the
course of the River Lostock to a bridge,
water splash (for the adventurous) and
picnic tables. Off to the right a short
distance at this point is the **park lake**,
which is home to numerous waterbirds,
including at some times of year more than
250 Canada geese. Cross the bridge and go
right, climbing briefly but steeply to follow
a field edge path to a **bridge** spanning the
M6 motorway, beyond which you descend
to a car park and the A49.

3 Turn right on a **cycle lane** to a light-
controlled crossing of the A6 at **Bamber**

Left: Cuerden Hall
Below left: Preston Junction Nature Reserve

2h30 · **13 MILES** · **20 KM** · **LEVEL 123**

Bridge. Go forward, still on a cycle lane, as far as **Church Road**, and there cross the road at a safe crossing point, and turn into **Havelock Road**. Follow the road, shortly passing a small **industrial estate** to meet another lane. Turn right, and go past a **supermarket** car park, turning right onto a cycle lane once more, and through a low **tunnel** (dismount here). Just beyond, turn left beneath a road bridge into the edge of a housing estate. At a T-junction turn right towards a roundabout, but cross, left, just before it to enter the **Preston Junction Local Nature Reserve**.

4 Follow a clear track to a road. Cross and keep forward to cross another back lane. Go forward along the middle one of three possibilities. After a short rise the towers of **Preston** come into view. Descend to cross a farm access track, and keep on to meet a gravel track along the edge of **woodland**.

5 When the gravel track forks, branch right, descending to a track junction beside the **River Ribble**. Turn right to the next bridge, and here bear right and left to gain the bridge, across which the **Miller and Avenham Parks** mark the end of the route. Across the parks the centre of Preston is soon reached.

6 Return by re-crossing the bridge, but instead of dipping down to the River Ribble, keep forward along an **avenue of trees** to meet the back lane crossed on the way out. Here rejoin the outward route, and retrace this first to **Bamber Bridge** and, once you have safely negotiated the A6, back into **Cuerden Valley Park** and on to Whittle-le-Woods.

MAP: OS Explorer 286 Blackpool and Preston

START/FINISH: Whittle-le-Woods, Chorley, down Factory Lane; grid ref: SD575217

TRAILS/TRACKS: good tracks, stony in places, or surfaced

LANDSCAPE: river valley park, small urban section, woodland

PUBLIC TOILETS: none on route

TOURIST INFORMATION: Chorley, tel: 01257 241693

CYCLE HIRE: none locally

THE PUB: Halfway House Hotel, Clayton-le-Woods

Getting to the start

Whittle-le-Woods is a suburb of Chorley, and lies along the A6, 2 miles (3.2km) north of the town. The start of the Cuerden Cycle Route is down Factory Lane in Whittle-le-Woods, just to the north of the church.

Why do this cycle ride?

Long stretches of traffic-free cycling through a wooded river valley are linked by safe cycling crossing points and cycle lanes into an old railway trackbed and then an even older tramway trackbed into city centre parks in Preston. The whole ride is through an intense area of habitat for a diverse range of flora and fauna. The ride can be shortened by taking a picnic as far as the bridge crossing in Cuerden Valley Park.

Researched and written by: Terry Marsh

Cuerden Valley

LANCASHIRE

Cuerden Valley LANCASHIRE

Preston Station

Preston

A6

River Ribble

B6230

M6

-N-

⑥

⑤

Mains House Farm

A675

Higher Walton

A675

River Darwen

Walton-le-Dale

Penwortham Lane

A6

B5258

Bamber Bridge

Jct 30

B5254

B5257

Tardy Gate

Lostock

River

A582

A6

④

Walton Summit

M61

Jct 2/9

Cuerden Green

P

③

Jct 29/1

M65

A6

Clayton Brook

A5083

Cuerden Hall

P

Cuerden Valley Park

Clayton Green

Farington

A49

M6

P

②

Halfway House Hotel

B5256

B5256

Jct 28

Clayton-le-Woods

M61

B5256

Leyland

START P

①

✝ Whittle-le-Woods

B5248

A49

B5248

0   1 mile

0   1km

Worden Park

Chorley ↓

A6

Halfway House Hotel

Reputedly at the exact 'halfway' point between London and Glasgow – hence its name – this modernised and comfortably refurbished roadside inn retains much of its former charm, when it was a favoured stopping point for charabancs bound for Blackpool and car travellers heading to and from Scotland. The traditionally furnished interior comprises a large lounge, dining room and a taproom with games area and the full range of Lees beers on tap. Note the lovely old sign on the gable entrance welcoming motorists and cyclists, a reminder of those early days of motoring and its time as a popular café for motorcyclists.

Food
Traditional pub food ranges from sausages and mash, pasta meals and lasagne to beef in black bean sauce. Sandwiches and light meals are also available.

Family facilities
Children can make good use of the outdoor play area in the beer garden on fine days. They are also welcome indoors and a children's menu is available.

Alternative refreshment stops
The ride passes near numerous restaurants, pubs and cafés in Preston and Chorley.

☛ Where to go from here
For a family fun outing that includes thrilling rides, jousting tournaments and spectacular magic shows, venture into King Arthur's Kingdom at Camelot Theme Park (www.camelotthemepark.co.uk) south of Leyland off the A49 near Charnock Richard. Astley Hall west of Chorley is a charming

about the pub

Halfway House Hotel
470 Preston Road, Clayton-le-Woods
Chorley, Lancashire PR6 7JB
Tel: 01772 334477

DIRECTIONS: beside the A6 a mile (1.6km) north of Factory Lane and the start of the ride
PARKING: 100
OPEN: daily; all day
FOOD: daily; all day
BREWERY/COMPANY: J W Lees Brewery
REAL ALE: J W Lees Bitter, Moonraker & seasonal beers
ROOMS: None available

Tudor/Stuart building set in beautiful parkland and retains a 'lived in' atmosphere. There are pictures and pottery to see, as well as fine furniture and rare plasterwork ceilings (www.lancashiretourism.com).

Calderdale and the Rochdale Canal

Take an easy towpath ride through West Yorkshire's industrial heritage.

The Rochdale Canal

Like most northern valleys, Calderdale used to be a swamp, choked with scrub alder trees. For centuries packhorse trains carried by Galloway ponies had tramped the Pennine high roads, linking the mill villages like Mankinholes, Heptonstall, and Sowerby. The Industrial Revolution changed all that. Fast transportation became the watchword as new heavy industries flourished. The valleys were cleared and drained, with new roads and towns built. The idea for the Rochdale Canal was first mooted in 1766 when James Brindley was asked to undertake a survey. It wasn't until 1794, 22 years after Brindley's death, that the necessary Act of Parliament was passed. The 33 mile (53km) canal, designed by William Jessop, would extend the existing Calder and Hebble Navigation through Todmorden and Rochdale to link with the Bridgewater Canal at Castlefield in Manchester. Upland reservoirs had to be constructed to feed the 92 locks before the first trans-Pennine canal opened in 1804.

The railways came. In 1841 George Stephenson surveyed and built a line parallel to the canal. Initially, the combination worked well and the annual goods passing through by barge had reached 686,000 tons. By the 20th century, however, the tonnage had declined. In 1952 the canal closed. Happily, that was not the end of the story, for the 1980s and 90s saw the restoration of the canal – this time for leisure activities.

the ride

1 There's access to the canal at the back of the car park where you turn left along the towpath, past old mill buildings. On the initial stages the shapely hill of **Stoodley Pike** and its obelisk monument looms large on the horizon. You'll see many houseboats moored on Veever's Wharf just outside the town – many have their own canalside gardens. Take care when rounding the canal locks hereabouts for the gates protrude across the towpath. High on a hillside to the left the gaunt soot-stained church at **Cross Stone** offers a stark contrast to the stone-built canalside terraces with their pretty cottage gardens. The River Calder closes in on the canal, and before long you find yourself cycling on a narrow tree-lined island between the two watercourses.

2 Just beyond **Holmcoat Lock No. 14** the towpath joins a tarred lane for a short stretch before descending back to the canalside. Take care here. At **Charlestown** pass the sewage works as quickly as possible! Just beyond the works the route is crossed by the Pennine Way long-distance path. For those in need of early refreshment, the towpath goes right by the **Stubbing Wharf pub**, which has tables outside in the summer, then the canal café. Next to the latter there's the Hebden Bridge Alternative Technology Centre.

3 On reaching Hebden Bridge proper you climb to and cross a **humpback bridge**, beyond which the towpath continues on the opposite bank, between the canal and a park (with toilets). However, you will probably wish to take a look around this

The Rochdale Canal flowing through the mill town of Hebden Bridge

4h00 — **18 MILES** — **29 KM** — **LEVEL 1**23

MAP: OS Explorer OL21 South Pennines

START/FINISH: Lever Street car park, Todmorden; grid ref: SD938241

TRAILS/TRACKS: narrow canal towpath

LANDSCAPE: mill towns, woodland and a semi-rural valley

PUBLIC TOILETS: the park at Hebden Bridge, and car park at Tuel Lock, Sowerby Bridge

TOURIST INFORMATION: Hebden Bridge, tel: 01422 843831

CYCLE HIRE: none locally

THE PUB: Shoulder of Mutton, Mytholmroyd
🛈 Unsuitable for small children. Take care under bridges: dismount if not confident. Permit needed to cycle towpaths (download from www.waterscape.com/cycling)

Getting to the start

Todmorden is at the junction of the A646 Burnley to Halifax Road and the A6033 to Rochdale. The car park is just east of the town centre along the Halifax Road. With your back to the town centre, turn right (south) along Union Street South, which leads to Lever Street Car Park. The railway runs parallel, with stations at Todmorden, Hebden Bridge, Mytholmroyd and Sowerby Bridge, so it is possible to cycle one way and get the train back.

Why do this cycle ride?

It's a ride through the history of the Industrial Revolution and transportation, past and present.

Researched and written by: John Gillham

pleasant mill town. This is also a good turning point for cyclists with limited time or with young children. The wharf here has been restored and is usually highlighted by smart, brightly coloured longboats.

4 A mile (1.6km) beyond the town the towpath climbs out to the busy Halifax road to avoid a short tunnel. It's best to get off here and cross carefully. There's a short track leading back to the canalside, which leads into **Mytholmroyd**. To get to the pub , leave the towpath and turn right along the road to the A road. Turn right again here, then left down New Road, signed 'to Cragg'.

5 Return to the towpath and continue past the **cricket club**. Beyond this there's a short but steady climb to reach a road near the apex of a bend. Cross with care and descend back to the towpath. You're back into the country again until **Luddenden Foot** where you'll need to get off to go down some steps in the towpath.

6 The towpath goes through the short **Hollins Mill Tunnel** where it's single file only. Give way to riders and walkers already in the tunnel. Beyond this you arrive at Sowerby Bridge. The **Tuel Lock** here is the deepest inland water lock in the UK. **Wainhouse Tower** is on the distant hill. Turn round and retrace your route back to the start or go back by train.

Calderdale WEST YORKSHIRE

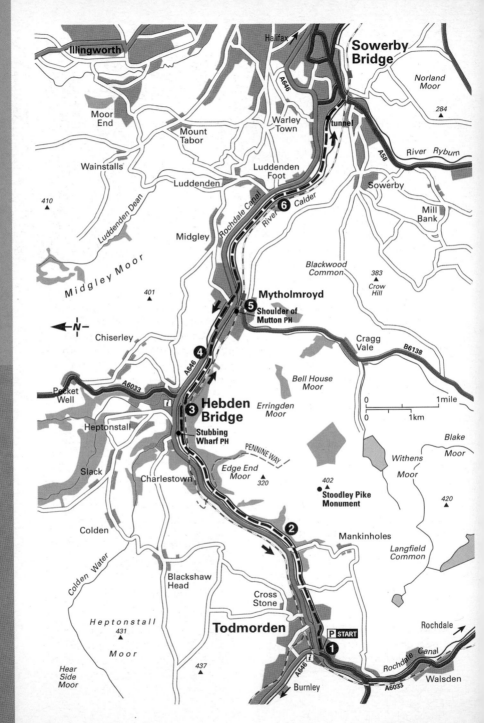

Shoulder of Mutton

A typical Pennines pub next to a trout stream, well situated for local walks and the popular Calderdale Way. It was associated with the infamous Crag Coiners, 18th-century forgers who made their own golden guineas. There's a display of memorabilia (coins and tools) relating to the Coiners above the fireplace in the spacious bar, which also features a rustic board and black-and-red tiled floor. There's a cosy, cottage-style dining room with low beams and dark wood furnishings, and a secure back yard for bikes.

Food

A menu featuring home-cooked dishes from fresh ingredients includes good-value snacks like sandwiches (served with chips), filled jacket potatoes and burger and chips. Main meals include beef in ale pie, Cumberland sausages, steak and onion pie, a daily roast from the carvery, and up to ten vegetarian dishes.

Family facilities

Children are welcome inside and smaller portions of dishes are readily available. Sheltered garden beside the trout stream.

Alternative refreshment stops

The Stubbing Wharf pub beside the canal near Hebden Bridge and the Canal Café at Hebden Bridge.

☛ Where to go from here

Drive up to see the attractive old weaving village of Heptonstall, above Hebden Bridge. Take the children to Eureka! The Museum for Children in Halifax, a fully interactive museum with over 400 'must touch' exhibits inviting you to take a journey of discovery through four main gallery spaces: Me and My Body, Living and Working Together, Our Global Garden and Invent, Create and Communicate (www.eureka.org.uk).

about the pub

Shoulder of Mutton
New Road, Mytholmroyd
Halifax, West Yorkshire HX7 5DZ
Tel: 01422 883165

DIRECTIONS:	On B6138 in Mytholmroyd, opposite the railway station
PARKING:	16
OPEN:	daily; all day Saturday and Sunday
FOOD:	no food Tuesday evening
BREWERY/COMPANY:	Enterprise Inns
REAL ALE:	Caledonian Deuchars IPA, Timothy Taylor Landlord, Flowers IPA, Black Sheep Bitter, guest beers

Around Rivington and its reservoir

Rivington's picturesque reservoir

Explore Lever Park and discover Lord Leverhulme's ruined castle.

Castles and barns

Liverpool Castle is an intentional ruin, built on a small hill, Cob Lowe, by Lord Leverhulme as a replica of the castle in Liverpool Bay. It overlooks the waters of Lower Rivington reservoir and has a fine view of Rivington Pike, one of Lancashire's best-known landmarks, part of a chain of beacon fires used to warn of danger. It was used at the time of the Spanish Armada in 1588.

Great House Barn is one of a small number of half-cruck barns in Lancashire, probably dating to Saxon times. Today it houses an information point, a gift shop and tea room open every day of the year, except Christmas Day. Originally, it would have been used to shelter cattle and feed. From the barn an imposing driveway leads up to Rivington Hall, formerly the home of the Lord of the Manor. It has a fine red-brick Georgian façade, and, like the barns, was probably built on a site of Saxon importance.

the ride

1 Leave from the bottom end of the car park, passing a **barrier** and soon, at a track junction, turn left, descending to cross a narrow, **wooded gully**. Follow a clear track, around a field edge, to another track junction at the edge of large open area. Bear

right and follow a clear track to **Liverpool Castle**. From the castle entrance, head down a long woodland drive to meet a road.

2 Turn right for 330yds (300m), passing a **school**. At the end of **metal railings**, turn left up a surfaced lane to a rough stony track on left, the lowest of three tracks at this junction. Follow this along an avenue of trees to another track junction, and there turn right, pass a **gate** onto a gently rising track. Continue forward at the next gate. When the track forks, bear left, and curve round left and right to a rough-surfaced lane beside **Rivington Hall**. Bear right to ride behind the hall into a car park.

3 Cross the car park, go forward past a wooden barrier and down a **stony driveway**, the right-hand of two exit drives. When the drive forks, bear right to a road. Emerge with care and turn right to pass **Rivington Stocks**, and going left with the main road. On reaching **Upper Rivington Reservoir**, leave the road by turning right onto a narrow road (bridleway).

Rivington Hall, built in the 18th century, is passed on the cycle route

1h30 — **7.5 MILES** — **12 KM** — **LEVEL 123**

MAP: OS Explorer 19 West Pennine Moors

START/FINISH: Great House Barn car park, Rivington; grid ref: SD628139

TRAILS/TRACKS: stony, woodland tracks and minor roads

LANDSCAPE: mainly woodland, some open areas around reservoirs

PUBLIC TOILETS: at start

TOURIST INFORMATION: Great House Barn (at the start)

CYCLE HIRE: none locally

THE PUB: The Millstone, Anderton

🛈 Some short ascents, and one long road climb

Getting to the start

Great House Barn lies within Lever Park, on the edge of Horwich. Accessible from Junction 8 on the M61 motorway, and then along the A6 through Chorley to Adlington on the A673, or from Junction 6, and then by A6027 and through Horwich on the A673.

Why do this cycle ride?

The wild uplands and string of reservoirs of the West Pennine Moors make fine habitats for flora and fauna alike, and provide a network of tracks, paths and trails for exploring. Lever Park, sometime property of Lord Leverhulme, where this ride begins, has at its centre the attractive village of Rivington and historical buildings like the Great House Barn, Rivington Hall and Liverpool Castle.

Researched and written by: Terry Marsh

Rivington

LANCASHIRE

4 Continue beside the reservoir (left) and a large pond (right) to a gate on the left giving onto a stony track up to **Yarrow Reservoir**. Follow the track to a road at a gate.

5 Turn left, downhill, and follow the road left and across the reservoir road, passing **The Yew Tree Inn**. Go down a dip

and up the long, steady ascent of **Nickelton Brow** to a T-junction. Go left into New Road.

6 Turn left again at **Horrobin Lane**. Go down and cross between reservoirs, and then take the first turning on the right, rising through a small car park onto a **woodland track**. As this forks, keep ahead (right), and soon return to the start.

Rivington LANCASHIRE

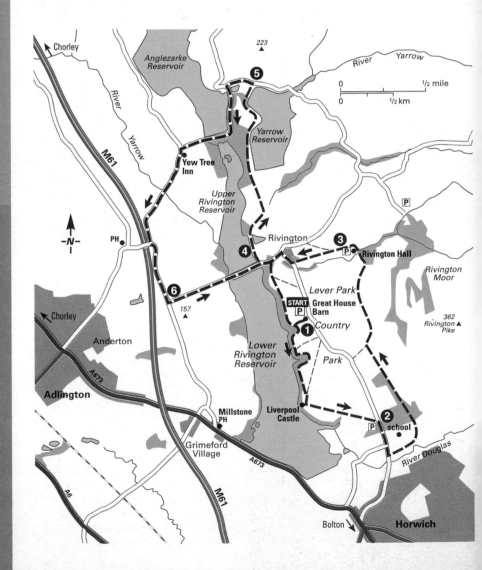

The Millstone

Occupying a glorious position overlooking Rivington Reservoir, the old Millstone pub has been stylishly converted into a contemporary bar-restaurant serving modern European food. Although, not really a 'pub' in the true sense of the word, you will find the atmosphere friendly and informal and the lunchtime menu light and good value. In addition, there's a splendid garden for summer eating and drinking, and it is a popular meeting place among local walking and cycling groups. It has a relaxing interior with wooden floors and wall panelling and a vibrant Mediterranean-style décor.

Food

Food is freshly prepared and takes in an imaginative range of eight pasta dishes among the lunchtime selection. Other dishes may include mustard and honey-glazed ham, roast lamb shank, and slow-roasted duck leg with sea salt and rosemary.

about the pub

The Millstone
Bolton Road, Anderton
Chorley, Lancashire PR6 9HJ
Tel: 01257 480205
www.sanrocco.co.uk

DIRECTIONS: on the A673, 1 mile (1.6km) north west of Horwich. Turn right from the car park to the A673 at Horwich and turn right for the pub

PARKING: 80

OPEN: all day Saturday & Sunday; closed Monday except Bank Holidays

FOOD: daily; all day Sunday

BREWERY/COMPANY: free house

REAL ALE: none served

Family facilities

Children are very welcome here and smaller portions of all main meals are available.

Alternative refreshment stops

Picnic sites on the ride, the Yew Tree Inn and restaurants in Horwich and Anderton.

☞ Where to go from here

North of Chorley stands the Hoghton Tower, a fortified 16th-century house with a fascinating history. It was here in 1617 that the sirloin steak came into being, when King James I famously knighted a loin of beef. Cedar Farm Galleries at Mawdesley, 6 miles (9.7km) east of Chorley, offers contemporary crafts, unique shops, a café, farm animals and a funky playground (www.lancashiretourism.com).

Rivington **LANCASHIRE**

Haigh Country Park

Visit the seat of the Earls of Balcarres and discover the woodlands of Haigh.

Haigh Hall

You can't go in, but Haigh Hall was previously the home of the Earl of Crawford and Balcarres, and is a listed building dating back to 1850. The nearby stable buildings have been converted to a small museum, café and gift shop, with a children's play area nearby. There's also a miniature railway, which operates during the summer months. Keep an eye open along the canal for birdlife, especially kingfishers which are more common here than might be imagined. Just on the edge of the estate, along Copperas Lane, is a small pond. It was formerly used for curling, and is known as the 'Curling Pond'. Kingfishers love the overhanging branches from which to feed.

the ride

1 Leave the car park and turn left (beware speed ramps), and follow a hedgerowed lane that soon starts to descend to a junction with the B5239. This B-road is well used, but there is a wide **footpath** on the right-hand side, which can be used, if necessary,

1h00 **6 MILES** **9.7 KM** **LEVEL 1 2 3**

to walk to the Leeds–Liverpool Canal. Follow the road to **traffic lights** controlling the narrow bridge spanning the canal.

2 Turn left onto the canal towpath at the **Crawford Arms** pub, and follow the tow path to an **iron trellis bridge** (No. 60) – take care on the small humpback bridge just before it. Here leave the towpath, and carry bikes up a few steps to meet the main **estate road** through Haigh.

3 Turn right, and after about 100 yards (91m), turn right again on a broad drive leading out to a gate, near a cottage, at the top of **Hall Lane**. Ride down the lane (rough in places, but motorable, and a popular way into the woodlands of Haigh). Approaching the River Douglas, Hall Lane takes a wide sweep down to the **bridge** spanning the river, from which it climbs to meet the A49, at a T-junction.

4 Go left, and, if necessary, walk the 200 yards (182m) to the main Wigan entrance to **Haigh Country Park**, passing through ornate iron gates. Follow the broad, descending track ahead, which soon crosses the Douglas. Bear right, following the main track as it curves around and begins the long, steady climb back up to the **Leeds–Liverpool Canal**, and then on to the straight drive leading directly to the front of **Haigh Hall**.

5 Keep to the right of the Hall, and go up the road behind it. **The Stables Centre**, café and shop, are on the right. The car park is directly ahead, just beyond the golf shop. Turn left into the car park to complete the ride.

The golf course at Haigh Country Park

MAP: OS Explorer 276 Bolton, Wigan and Warrington

START/FINISH: Haigh Country Park; grid ref: SD596088

TRAILS/TRACKS: canal towpath, surfaced estate or traffic roads. Stretch of 220yds (200m) on a wide town road, which can be walked. There are no cycle trails within Haigh Country Park; cyclists are asked to use the roads and trails with care for other users

LANDSCAPE: woodland, farmland and canal towpath

PUBLIC TOILETS: Stables Centre, near start

TOURIST INFORMATION: Wigan Pier, tel: 01942 825677

CYCLE HIRE: none locally

THE PUB: Balcarres Arms, Haigh

🔴 One long, steady climb. Beware speed ramps on estate roads and care to be taken alongside the canal

Getting to the start
Haigh Country Park is within easy reach of both the M6 (Junction 27) and the M61 (Junction 6). From the M6, take the A49 towards Standish, then the B5239 to Haigh. Look out for the B5239 and Aspull, then Haigh, when leaving the M61. In Haigh, turn down Copperas Lane, near the Balcarres Arms, to reach the car park.

Why do this cycle ride?
Haigh Country Park has many attractions for children and the woodlands have great appeal plus almost 100 species of birds during the year. The Leeds to Liverpool Canal through the park provides an excellent opportunity to explore.

Researched and written by: Terry Marsh

The sweeping driveway and symmetrical façade of Haigh Hall

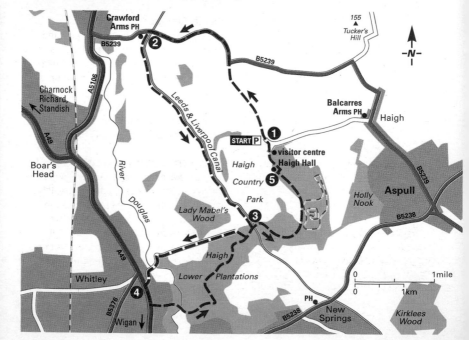

Balcarres Arms

Named after the Earl of Balcarres, who lived at nearby Haigh Hall, this is an unpretentious pub of some antiquity tucked away in historic Haigh, close to Haigh Country Park. Very much a locals' haunt, it is simply furnished and decorated and comprises a main bar and a cosy snug bar, and serves unfussy, home-cooked pub food.

Food
Expect sandwiches and light lunchtime snacks alongside home-made minted lamb casserole, Cock 'n' Bull (chicken and beef in a creamy pepper sauce), beef Madras and a range of vegetarian meals like vegetable lasagne and aubergine moussaka.

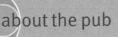 about the pub

Balcarres Arms
1 Copperas Lane, Haigh
Wigan, Lancashire WN2 1PA
Tel: 01942 833377

DIRECTIONS: beside the Country Park access road in Haigh village, 0.5 mile (800m) from the start point of the ride	
PARKING: 50	
OPEN: daily; all day	
FOOD: daily	
BREWERY/COMPANY: Wolverhampton & Dudley	
REAL ALE: Cockerhoop, guest ale	

Family facilities
Children are allowed inside the pub until 9pm and there's a standard children's menu for younger family members. There is a garden with picnic benches for summer alfresco eating and drinking.

Alternative refreshment stops
The Stables café at the end of the route.

☛ Where to go from here
Head for Wigan Pier for a journey never to be forgotten. Part museum, part theatre, it is a mixture of entertainment and education. Step back in time at 'The Way We Were' heritage centre, visit Trencherfield Mill and the Machinery Hall, and then visit the Opie's Museum of Memories. There is loads going on, including walks, talks, boat trips, events and much more.

The Upper Don Valley Trail

Exploring a valley emerging from an industrial past.

Trans-Pennine Trail

As numerous signs indicate, this route is part of the Trans-Pennine Trail. Described as the country's first multi-user long-distance route, it is open to walkers and cyclists throughout its length, with large sections also available to horse-riders and wheelchair users. The full distance, coast to coast, is 215 miles (346km), with extensions and branches adding up to a grand total of 350 miles (563km). The Trail is also part of the National Cycle Network and links to the E8 European long-distance path, which will eventually stretch all the way from the west coast of Ireland to Istanbul.

A stone's throw from the start is the eastern entrance to the Woodhead Tunnels. The first single-track tunnel was completed in 1845, with a second bore added in 1852. It is claimed that three per cent of the labourers working on the original tunnel lost their lives. Almost exactly 3 miles (4.8km) long, the original tunnels, from which smoke and fumes never cleared, were also unpopular with train crews on the open footplates of the steam engines. The line was part of the Great Central Railway, and later the London & North Eastern Railway before the railways were nationalised. A third, twin-track tunnel opened in 1953 and the line was electrified the following year. However, passenger traffic ceased in 1970 and the line finally closed in 1981.

Top: The Upper Don Valley Trail near Oxspring

the ride

1 From the bottom of the car park go through barriers and out on to the obvious trail. Bear right and drop down slightly on to the main line of the **old railway trackbed**. There is a sort of 'dual-carriageway' structure, with the intention being that the left-hand side is for cyclists and walkers, the right for horses. Even when there are no horses to be seen, 'their' side can be rougher (and pose certain other hazards!). Once past the **old station platforms**, the surroundings open out, with moorland up to the right. Go under the bridge on to a narrower section – single carriageway – and continue to **Hazlehead**. The old station buildings have now been converted into a private residence.

2 A bridge takes you over the A616. Pass a couple of smaller bridges and emerge on to a short elevated section. On the right, some obvious diggings are part of the old **Bullhouse colliery**. The most obvious feature is the **settlement lagoon**, part of a project to improve water quality of the river (a signboard explains all).

3 Pass some industrial buildings and a **wind turbine** on the colliery site, and cross a bridge above the A628. After a more open stretch, cross a lane. The barriers are tricky for adults to negotiate but small children can ride straight under them, so watch for traffic. Another track crosses the route and then an alternation of cuttings and open sections leads to a **recreation ground**, complete with skateboard park, on the outskirts of Penistone.

4 This section inevitably has a more urban feel but for the most part is surprisingly well insulated. Pass an **old engine shed** on the right, then go over a bridge, overlooked by the tower of the village church. Another cutting and another bridge lead to the overgrown platforms of **Penistone station**. Just beyond is the still-active railway line linking Huddersfield and Barnsley, with the current station away to the left. Follow the cycle trail alongside the railway line for about 0.5 mile (800m).

5 The railway swings away and the trail continues to pass under another bridge on the outskirts of **Oxspring**. At this point the trail divides. The left branch goes towards Barnsley, presently joining the Dove Valley Trail (see Ride 24). If you don't want to go the full distance, you can follow this route down to the main road and a short way right to the Waggon and Horses at Oxspring.

6 Otherwise, keep straight ahead in the direction of Sheffield. Negotiate more barriers to cross a **farm track** and then cross a bridge high above the **River Don**. A sign warns of the tunnel ahead and then the cutting closes in. The trail may be muddy here, and the air can be considerably colder too. The **tunnel** itself is well lit but still has a certain gloomy atmosphere. From its far end continue for about 600yds (549m), cross a bridge over a lane and reach some picnic tables. Drop down to the lane here and follow it left, under the trail, to reach the **Bridge Inn**. Once refreshed, you can retrace your tyre-tracks to the start. If you don't want to go back through the tunnel there is a waymarked alternative route.

3h00 — **20 MILES** — **32.2 KM** — **LEVEL 1 2 3**

SHORTER ALTERNATIVE ROUTE

1h30 — **8.75 MILES** — **14.1 KM** — **LEVEL 1 2 3**

MAP: OS Explorer OL1 Dark Peak

START/FINISH: car park at Dunford Bridge; grid ref: SE158024

TRAILS/TRACKS: old railway track, mostly well-drained, occasionally muddy near far end point 1

LANDSCAPE: moorland, pastoral valley, woodland and some urban fringe

PUBLIC TOILETS: portaloo at start

TOURIST INFORMATION: Holmfirth, tel: 01484 222444

CYCLE HIRE: The Bike Shed, Scissett, Huddersfield, tel: 0800 018 4753

THE PUB: Bridge Inn, Thurgoland

🛈 Moderately steep ascent and descent on lane to pub at far point

Getting to the start

From Holmfirth, head south on B6106 for about 1.5 miles (2.4km) to Longley, fork right through Hade Edge and follow the road past several reservoirs into the Don valley. Large car park on the left just before the bridge.

Why do this cycle ride?

The Upper Don Valley Trail follows the former main line between Sheffield and Manchester. In its entirety, this is a long ride, and it's downhill all the way to Thurgoland – so it's uphill all the way back. The gradient is always gentle but it is persistent. Those looking for a shorter outing can turn round anywhere, but an obvious place to do so is on the outskirts of Penistone.

Researched and written by: Jon Sparks

Upper Don Valley

SOUTH YORKSHIRE

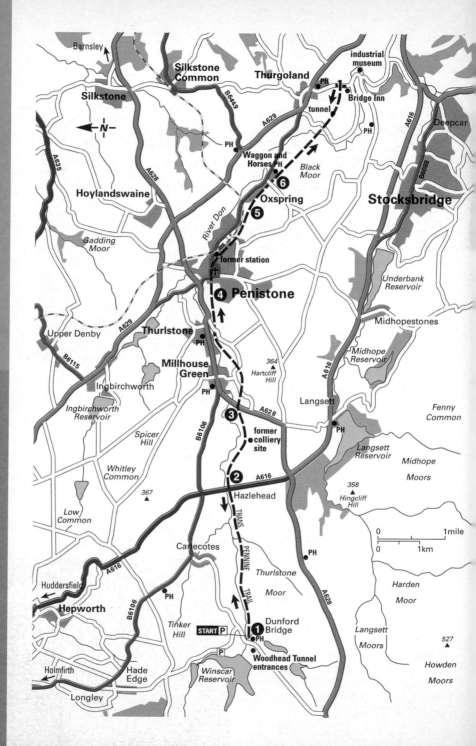

Barnsley

Silkstone
Common

Thurgoland

industrial
museum

PH

Bridge Inn

tunnel

PH

Silkstone

B6449

A629

Deepcar

A616

A635

PH

A628

Waggon and
Horses PH

Black
Moor

Stocksbridge

Hoylandswaine

6

B6088

River Don

Oxspring

5

Gadding
Moor

Underbank
Reservoir

former station

Midhopestones

A629

4 Penistone

Upper Denby

Thurlstone

PH

Midhope
Reservoir

A616

B6115

Millhouse
Green

364
Hartcliff
Hill

Ingbirchworth

PH

Langsett

Fenny
Common

Ingbirchworth
Reservoir

B6106

3

A628

PH

Langsett
Reservoir

Midhope
Moors

Spicer
Hill

former
colliery
site

Whitley
Common

2

A616

358
Hingcliff
Hill

367
▲

Hazlehead

Low
Common

0   1mile

0   1km

Carlecotes

TRANS

PH

A616

Thurlstone
Moor

Harden
Moor

Huddersfield

B6106

PENNINE

A628

Hepworth

PH

Tinker
Hill

START P

1

Dunford
Bridge

PH

TRAIL

Langsett
Moors

527
▲

Holmfirth

Hade
Edge

P

Woodhead Tunnel
entrances

Howden
Moors

Winscar
Reservoir

Longley

Bridge Inn

about the pub

Bridge Inn
Cote Lane, Thurgoland
Sheffield, South Yorkshire S35 7AE
Tel: 01142 2882016

DIRECTIONS: beside the River Don, 0.5 mile (800m) south of the village centre and the A629	
PARKING: 30	
OPEN: daily; all day	
FOOD: no food Sunday evening	
BREWERY/COMPANY: Enterprise Inns	
REAL ALE: Tetley, guest beer	

You have to leave the railway track to get to the Bridge Inn, but only for about 500yds (457m) of quiet lane – and there's the added novelty of being able to freewheel as you drop down slightly into the valley of the Don. In fact, if the weather is fine and you sit in the sheltered garden behind the pub, the loudest sound you'll hear is often the ripple of the river. Inside, a friendly welcome awaits. It's also useful to know that this solid stone-built pub Is a very short distance from the Wortley Top Forge Industrial Museum.

Food
From a printed menu order crusty baguettes, starters like home-made soup, Greek salad and deep-fried mushrooms, and traditional main dishes such as large battered haddock and chips, gammon, egg and chips, steak and ale pie, venison sausages and mash, lasagne with garlic ciabatta, or rump steak with all the trimmings. Daily specials board.

Family facilities
Children are very welcome in the pub and a standard children's menu is available. Secluded and safe rear garden for summer eating and drinking.

Alternative refreshment stops
For those preferring to undertake the slightly shorter ride, the Waggon and Horses at Oxspring is a good refreshment stop. It is open all day and welcomes children (menu). There are also several pubs and cafés in Penistone.

☛ Where to go from here
Wortley Top Forge Industrial Museum (www.topforge.co.uk).

The Dove Valley Trail

Rural surprises to be found in the heart of industrial South Yorkshire.

Wentworth Castle

Wentworth Castle is conspicuous soon after Point 3. Those doing the return through the lanes will pass much closer to it, but see little of the castle itself. They will, however, see some of the associated estate buildings. The present castle is largely the result of a massive programme of works in the early 18th century, instigated by Sir Thomas Wentworth, Earl of Strafford. He originally expected to inherit the estate at Wentworth Woodhouse, a few miles away, but it went to a cousin instead. Much of the motivation for all the grand works around Wentworth Castle seems to have been a burning desire to outshine his cousin's property. The castle is now home to the Northern College for Residential Adult Education. It is a Grade I listed building, but is probably less important than the surrounding gardens and parkland. These contain a fine iron conservatory and mock Gothic castle, which gained greater public prominence during the first (2003) series of the BBC2 programme *Restoration*, ultimately achieving third place in the final. The gardens are open to the public at limited times, mostly on weekend afternoons.

the ride

1 From the corner of the car park furthest from the road, a path leads via a ramp to a lane. Follow this right and

down, then bear right before the **museum** and down past the **Field Study Centre**. Go over a couple of small bridges then turn left, with a sign to the Trans Pennine Trail. Follow the narrow track, rising quite steeply, keep straight ahead on tarmac, and finally go up alongside a gate to the **railway track** and turn left.

2 There's a short tree-lined section then it opens out, with views over the reservoir on the left. On the other side a short track and the crossing of a lane give access to **Wigfield Open Farm** and its café. Follow the rail track to a barrier. Go straight across the lane to the continuation of the track, alongside a small **car park**.

3 The surroundings are now pleasantly rural, but your ears tell you that the M1 is not far off. High on the left beyond the motorway is the impressive façade of **Wentworth Castle**. After a slightly narrower section, negotiate more barriers at the crossing of a narrow tarmac lane – or you can take the mountain bikers' route over humps. Soon after this you come out on to the **iron bridge** over the M1. High parapets, embellished with fine graffiti art, conceal the motorway from view. And very quickly, depending on wind direction, the noise fades.

4 Continue along the narrow trail through **young woods**, the trees meeting overhead in places. After crossing a sandy track, with more barriers, there's an open area, with masses of ragwort, **picnic tables**, and regular glimpses of open fields.

A sculpture on the Dove Valley Trail

2h00 — **9 MILES** — **14.5 KM** — **LEVEL 123**

SHORTER ALTERNATIVE ROUTE

1h30 — **8.25 MILES** — **13.3 KM** — **LEVEL 123**

MAP: OS Explorer 278 Sheffield & Barnsley

START/FINISH: Worsbrough Country Park car park; grid ref: SE352033

TRAILS/TRACKS: old railway tracks and short surfaced tracks through country park; alternative return on lanes

LANDSCAPE: reservoir and valley with mix of farmland and woodland

PUBLIC TOILETS: at Worsbrough Mill

TOURIST INFORMATION: Barnsley, tel: 01226 206757

CYCLE HIRE: Cycosport, Barnsley, tel: 01226 204020

THE PUB: Button Mill Inn, Barnsley

🛈 Some steep climbs and descents on return through lanes

Getting to the start

Leave the M1 at junction 36 and follow the A61 towards Barnsley. The Worsbrough Country Park car park is on the left as the road descends into the valley of the River Dove.

Why do this cycle ride?

This ride starts on the edge of Barnsley, and crosses the M1, so you might not expect to find peace and quiet, but the surroundings are almost entirely rural. It makes for a gentle ride, ideal for younger children, especially with the country park and open farm near the start. The more ambitious can take on the return through the lanes, which doesn't add much to the distance but does include a steep climb and descent.

Researched and written by: Jon Sparks

Dove Valley

SOUTH YORKSHIRE

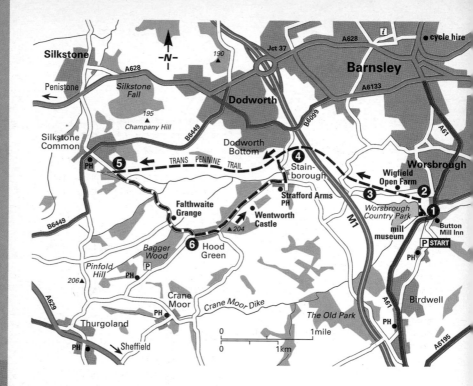

The track now begins to climb discernibly, and an elevated section takes you through more mature woods. Just before a bridge, with a road below, watch for a sign showing a cyclist, a pedestrian and a **British Rail symbol**. (It's possible to continue a little further but soon the line is blocked, before it enters the Silkstone tunnel. The Trans Pennine Trail continues from this point by the 'up and over path'.)

5 Either turn back along the rail track or follow the sign down a ramp to a lane and turn left. Descend past **Nabs Wood** (Woodland Trust) on the right, make a short climb, and swing left at the top of the rise, enjoying the more open views. Drop down again, go over the bridge and then climb once more. It soon eases off. Pass some fine, recently restored timber-framed buildings at **Falthwaite Grange**, keep left at a small

junction, and then a slight dip leads all too quickly into a very steep but not too long climb past **Bagger Wood** and into the village of **Hood Green**. At a T-junction where the road levels off, turn left.

6 At the far end of the village there's another short steep rise. Keep left at a junction. Continue through **woodland** with steep slopes dropping to the left, then descend quite steeply, into the village of **Stainborough**. As the road begins to level out there's a crossroads. (The alternative pub, the **Strafford Arms**, is a short way up to the right here.) Turn left and descend some more. Swing left by the entrance to **Strafford Industrial Park** then immediately fork right on to a rough track. This gets very rough on the final rise before rejoining the **old railway** at a Trans Pennine Trail sign. Turn right here to head back to the start.

Button Mill Inn

about the pub

Button Mill Inn
Park Road, Worsbrough Bridge
Barnsley, South Yorkshire S70 5LJ
Tel: 01226 282639

DIRECTIONS: see Getting to the Start; pub opposite the Country Park car park

PARKING: 40

OPEN: daily; all day

FOOD: daily; all day

BREWERY/COMPANY: FGL Pubs

REAL ALE: John Smiths's Bitter & Magnet

ROOMS: 7 en suite

Button Mill Inn couldn't be much more handily placed, just across the road from the car park (but cross with care, as it's a busy highway). It's a handsome, four-square sort of building, originally a coaching inn, dating from the 1840s, though today's interior has a more standardised pub feel to it. There's plenty of space, but it's broken into more manageable areas, helped by some small changes of level, and there is lots of comfortable seating, so overcrowding should rarely be a problem. A wide-ranging menu is served all day. One drawback is that the outside seating is a bit limited: the tables at the front are very close to the busy road, while there are a few more tables to be found at the back adjoining the car park.

Food
Food is traditional pub fare ranging from filled jacket potatoes and hot and cold sandwiches, to daily specials like duck in plum sauce, braised lamb shoulder and spicy beef fillet cooked Szechuan style.

Family facilities
Children are welcome in the bars and there is a children's menu available for younger family members.

Alternative refreshment stops
Café at Wigfield Open Farm and the Strafford Arms in Stainborough (just off the longer loop).

☛ Where to go from here
In addition to exploring Worsbrough Country Park and Mill Museum and the Wigfield Open Farm, take a look at the magnificent gardens at Wentworth Castle (www.wentworthcastle.org).

Wharncliffe Woods

A taste of mountain biking in a hotbed of the sport.

Wharncliffe Woods

Mountain biking is a relatively young sport, its origins usually traced to California in the late 1970s. It has grown hugely in popularity and cross-country racing has been an Olympic discipline since 1996. But it's the downhill variety for which Wharncliffe Woods is most notable. Double World Cup downhill champion Steve Peat learned his trade in this area and has subsequently been among those responsible for the construction of some fearsome routes here. Serious downhillers require some highly specialised gear, including body protection and full-face helmets. The bikes, too, are specialised, with beefed-up suspension front and rear and powerful disc brakes. There is also a sub-sport known as freeride, which involves tackling the biggest possible jumps and drop-offs.

The Wharncliffe Woods area has been subject to quarrying for millennia, with evidence of Iron Age activity on Wharncliffe Crags; in fact the name Wharncliffe derives from the word 'quern', which is a small hand-operated grindstone mostly used in grinding grain for flour. The rock is, of course, millstone grit. The crags are now popular with rock-climbers. Later the woods were managed to provide fuel for the iron industry that flourished in the Don Valley from the 16th century onwards. Today Forest Enterprise continues to extract some timber commercially but the woods are increasingly managed for amenity and conservation and areas have been planted with broad-leaved native trees such as oak and birch.

the ride

1 From the car park turn left along the broad trail. At a collection of **signposts** turn right and then duck under a barrier on the left on to a narrower path. After another barrier the trail becomes broader again, descending gently through attractive **woods** of oak and birch. Negotiate another barrier and turn right on a track that descends more steeply. At the bottom of a particularly steep section is a **3-way bridleway sign**.

2 Turn right, and continue through more downhill sections. Cross a small wooden bridge, and duck under a barrier, back into **Wharncliffe Woods** proper.

3 Turn left and continue downhill, swinging right on to a more gently descending section of track. At a fork bear left, emerge on to a broad track, and immediately fork right, passing a Trans Pennine Trail sign for **Wortley**. Continue downhill, taking great care on a section with a very loose surface where another track joins from the left. As a second track comes in from the left, look up to the right and you can see the first of the **MTB downhill routes** emerging on to the main track.

4 Now there's a slight climb followed by some gentle undulations, bringing you into a densely wooded section and coming close to a **railway line** on the left. After more level riding there's a fork, with a **Trans Pennine Trail sign**. Follow this down the broader left branch, swinging back right and rising where a narrower track forks off to the left. Now begin a long gentle ascent,

Below: Wharncliffe Woods

which dips under power lines. Look out for **Wharncliffe Crags** on the right through the trees before a slight dip. The track levels out for a short way. When it begins to climb again look for a sharp right turn just beyond another Trans Pennine Trail sign. There are also signs for **Wharncliffe Heath nature reserve** to look out for.

5 The climb isn't excessively steep anywhere, but some sections are made really tricky by the surface, which is either loose sand, loose stones or a mixture. Anyone who completes the ascent without dismounting can claim to have passed the entry exam to real mountain biking. Keep straight on through a gap in a wall and along a more level sandy track, now with open **moorland** on the right and some fine mature **oak woods** on the left. After another short ascent, meet a slightly wider track and continue straight ahead. Just beyond this the path levels out, with the most expansive views of the entire ride. As you come back into woods, the track dips down, with quite a tricky section over rocks and mud, to a road.

1h30 · **7 MILES** · **11.3 KM** · **LEVEL 123**

MAP: OS Explorer 278 Sheffield & Barnsley

START/FINISH: Wharncliffe Woods car park; grid ref: SK325951

TRAILS/TRACKS: mostly good forest tracks with a few narrower and/or rougher sections

LANDSCAPE: mature woodland, mostly coniferous plantations, with occasional views of farmland, heathland and crags

PUBLIC TOILETS: none on route

TOURIST INFORMATION: Sheffield, tel: 01142 211900

CYCLE HIRE: Cycosport, Barnsley, tel: 01226 204020

THE PUB: The Wortley Arms Hotel, Wortley

🛈 Some steep climbs and descents; beware some loose surfaces. For older, experienced children; mountain bike essential

Getting to the start

From M1 junction 36, follow the A61 towards Sheffield for 1.5 miles (2.4km), over a roundabout. Take the next right turn to Howbrook. Go left at the crossroads in the village. Follow this lane for about 0.5 mile (800m), crossing the A629, to reach a T-junction. Go left and in about 2 miles (3.2km) reach the main parking area for Wharncliffe Woods (on the right).

Why do this cycle ride?

Wharncliffe Woods is a name that dedicated mountain bikers recognise. Competitions are regularly held here. Our route doesn't involve anything extreme, but it does give a little of the flavour, with some fairly steep but well-surfaced descents, and a challenging climb. For a more straightforward ride, follow the green waymarked route from the car park.

Researched and written by: Jon Sparks

Wharncliffe Woods

SOUTH YORKSHIRE

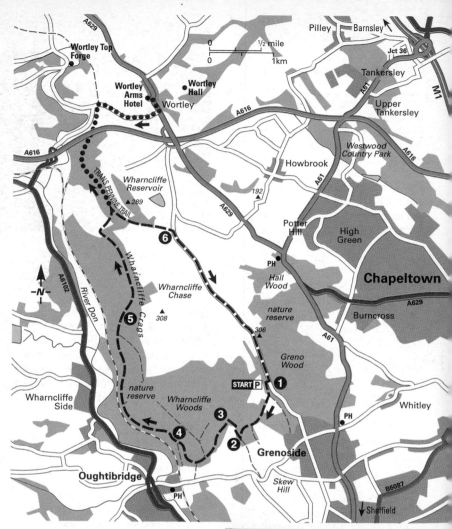

0   ½ mile

0   1km

–N–

6 Turn right and follow the road up a long gentle ascent. At the crest of the climb, coming back to **woods** on the right, another **Trans Pennine Trail sign** indicates a track that leads back to the car park.

There's no pub right on the ride route, though it could fairly easily be extended by continuing along the Trans Pennine Trail for about another mile (1.6km); pass under the A616 then soon after drop down to a minor road and follow it east to the A629. Turn left into Wortley.

The Wortley Arms Hotel

The landlord of this rambling old village pub is well used to cyclists and walkers. The pub is an official Trans Pennine Trail Stamping Point (anyone riding or walking the full coast-to-coast route can obtain a card and get it stamped at various points along the route). Also, since it was formerly known as The Wharncliffe Arms, there couldn't be a much more appropriate choice for this ride. It's a solid stone building that was built on the site of an earlier hostelry in 1754, with the arms of the Earls of Wharncliffe carved in stone over the door. Many of the old materials were used in the construction and inside you can see some fine wood panelling, exposed stonework, wooden floors and low beams, while in the lounge bar there's a huge inglenook fireplace with a log fire in winter.

Food

The lounge bar menu lists good traditional pub food. Choices include an extensive list of sandwiches and baguettes, various salads and filled jacket potatoes, and main dishes such as cod and chips, steak and ale pie and a roast of the day.

Family facilities

Children are welcome in the bars. There are no play facilities but young children do have their own menu.

Alternative refreshment stops

None on the route. Plenty of hotels, cafés, pubs and restaurants in Sheffield.

☛ Where to go from here

Sheffield has much to offer the family. Visit Kelham Island Museum for the story of Sheffield, its industry and life (www.simt.co.uk), the Fire and Police Museum or the Sheffield Bus Museum. Nearer Wharncliffe and Wortley is Wortley Top Forge (www.topforge.co.uk), the last example of a working water-powered drop forge. You can also look round Wortley Hall Gardens.

about the pub

The Wortley Arms Hotel

Halifax Road, Wortley
Sheffield, South Yorkshire S35 7DB
Tel: 01142 888749

DIRECTIONS: turn left from Wharncliffe Woods car park. At the junction of the A616 and A629, follow the A629 north for 0.5 mile (800m) to Wortley. Pub in village centre

PARKING: 30

OPEN: daily; all day

FOOD: daily; all day Saturday, Sunday until 6.30pm

BREWERY/COMPANY: free house

REAL ALE: Wortley Golden Best, Oakwell Barnsley Bitter, Black Sheep Bitter, Timothy Taylor Landlord, guest beers

ROOMS: 3 en suite

Acknowledgements

The Automobile Association would like to thank the following photographers, companies and picture libraries for their assistance in the preparation of this book.

Abbreviations for the picture credits are as follows: - (t) top; (b) bottom; (l) left; (r) right; (c) centre; (AA) AA World Travel Library.

Front cover AA/T Mackie; back cover AA/M Kipling; 3 AA/T Mackie; 6/7 AA; 12 AA/R Coulam; 13 AA/J Beazley; 15 Beadnell Towers Hotel; 17 AA/R Coulam; 18 AA/R Coulam; 19 AA; 20/21 AA/R Coulam; 22 AA/R Coulam; 23 AA/R Ireland; 24/25 AA/J Morrison; 27 AA/G Rowatt; 28 AA/D Tarn; 31 AA/J Sparks; 32 AA/J Morrison; 34 AA/J Morrison; 35 AA/J Gillham; 38 AA/J Morrison; 39 AA/J Gillham; 40 AA/P Bennett; 42 AA/J Morrison; 43 AA/J Morrison; 44 AA/J Gillham; 47 AA; 48/49 AA/T Marsh; 51 AA/T Marsh; 52/53 AA/T Marsh; 53t AA/T Marsh; 55 AA/T Marsh; 56 L Whitwam; 59 AA/J Gillham; 60 AA/J Gillham; 63 AA/J Morrison; 64bl AA/T Marsh; 64/65 AA/T Marsh; 67 AA/T Marsh; 68/69 AA/T Marsh; 70 AA/T Marsh; 71 AA/T Marsh; 73 AA/P Wilson; 74 AA/J Gillham; 75 AA/J Gillham; 77 AA/J Morrison; 79 AA/J Morrison; 80 AA/J Morrison; 83 AA/J Sparks; 84 AA/T Marsh; 85 AA/T Marsh; 87 AA/T Marsh; 89 L Whitwam; 91 AA/J Gillham; 92 AA/D Forss; 93 AA/D Forss; 95 AA/T Marsh; 96 AA/T Marsh; 98 AA/T Marsh; 99 AA/T Marsh; 100/101 AA/J Morrison; 102tl AA/J Sparks; 102br AA/J Morrison; 104 AA/J Sparks; 107 AA/J Sparks; 109 AA/J Morrison; 110 AA/J Morrison; 111 AA/J Morrison

Every effort has been made to trace the copyright holders, and we apologise in advance for any accidental errors. We would be happy to apply the corrections in the following edition of this publication.